The Dilly Deli Guide and Cookbook

The Dilly Deli Guide and Cookbook
by Kevin Leonard

Greatlakes Living Press, Publishers, Matteson, Illinois

The Dilly Deli Guide and Cookbook
©Kevin Leonard 1976
All rights reserved
Printed in U.S.A.
International Standard Book Number: 0-915498-28-6
Library of Congress Catalog Card Number: 76-42012

Greatlakes Living Press
3634 W. 216th Street
Matteson, Illinois 60443

Cover design by Joseph Mistak, Jr.
Cover photo by Patrick K. Snook and Jerry Trehan
Illustrations by Jack Haesly
Other design by Chris Avers

Credits

The author expresses appreciation to the following individuals and companies for the recipes they contributed:

Carl Buddig & Co., Chicago, Ill.
Herbert G. Lowinger, Chicago, Ill.
The National Kraut Packers Association, St. Charles, Ill.
Pickle Packers International, Inc., St. Charles, Ill.
Bob Protzel, St. Louis, Mo.
Fred Usinger, Inc., Milwaukee, Wis.
Vienna Sausage Mfg. Company, Chicago, Ill.
Max Shapiro, Indianapolis, Ind.

Contents

To Krissy, Cissy, Judi
and their Grandma Loretta,
who introduced them to
hot, steaming bagels when
they visited her
in Jackson Heights

Eppis Essen or, the Best of the Wurst

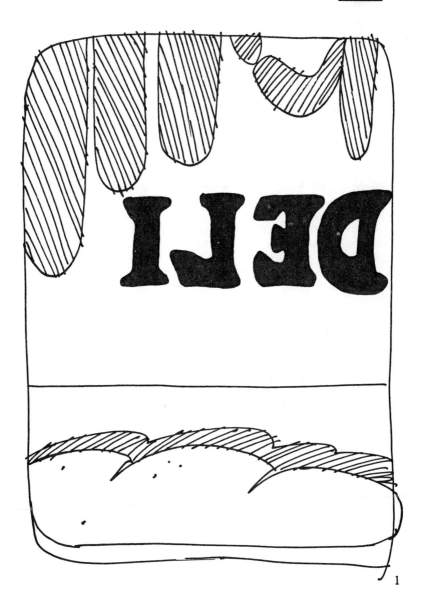

How did it all start? I'll tell you. The Crusaders noshed on sausages, and pastrami probably preceded Vlad the Impaler in Transylvania.

Centuries later, Isaac Gellis, with *wurstfabrik* experience in Berlin, emigrated to the United States and became a supplier of meat to the Union Army during the Civil War.

In 1872 he opened a sausage factory and meat processing plant at 37 Essex Street on New York's Lower East Side. Occasionally in the smoking process a large piece of meat would split into smaller segments. These Mr. Gellis would offer for sale at retail. Thus was born the delicatessen.

These legendary-sounding facts are corroborated by someone who really ought to know the territory — Isaac's grandson Abe Gellis, executive vice president of Isaac Gellis Inc., still purveying kosher provisions to New York and the nation. (And featured recently in "The Sunshine Boys.")

Isaac Gellis' show business connections go way back. The company has preserved an ancient postcard received by Eddie Cantor: "Murder will out. I found out here in Miami that you used to deliver salamis, pastramis and corned beef for Isaac Gellis ... The industry lost a great delivery boy." It's signed by Al Jolson.

What was it that Isaac Gellis introduced to America? Grandson Abe offers this bit of deli lore from the company's promotion files:

"We live in a world today where changes come so fast that encyclopedias have to be made with loose-leaf bindings. What happened last year is already ancient history ... and there's nothing deader than yesterday's newspaper.

"This chameleon complex affects our personal lives as well. Milady becomes a decided blonde ... in a split-second decision. Minks went along for a hundred centuries with their usual coloring until somebody on Seventh or Eighth Avenue dreamed up those sky-blue-pink mutations. East side kids who worked their way through night school now have scions who go to Ivy League colleges and play polo.

"But here's a funny thing. Your wife's taste in clothes can move

uptown from the Square to 57th Street. You can graduate from a railroad flat to a Westchester estate with an outdoor Dining Patio ... and four bathrooms *inside!* It's been a long time since your lunch was a frankfurter and a cup of tea (for a total of seven cents) at Max's Busy Bee. You are now on familiar terms with caviar, truffles and Guinea Hen under glass. But there's one thing that you don't forget.

"You never outgrow that yen for a juicy hot corned beef sandwich ... make it lean, Mr. Gellis, and an extra piece pickle, please.

"Your taste buds tingle poignantly every time you remember the seductive flavor of smooth, soft, spice-blessed Salami.

"And if you happen to pass a Gellis Delicatessen and get a heavenly whiff of that aromatic Pastrami ... you'll shed your gastronomic veneer and duck in for a Hot Pastrami Sandwich and a bottle of Celery Tonic.

"DON'T FIGHT IT! This craving for that old Gellis *'tom'* is bigger than the both of us. It's something that goes back to the cement-roots of New York (who had grass?) ... something that your great-grandfather knew before you.

"It goes back to the days when unexpected company meant a rare treat ... when Momma hurried you out to the nearest Gellis store to get me please a pound Salami, a half corned beef, thin sliced, and a quarter tongue ... don't let him give you the end!

"It goes back to the days when the semi-annual outing to Coney Island was a big event; the whole family elbowed its way onto subway or trolley, laden with bathing gear and a lunch-bundle bulging with delicatessen sandwiches (what else was so handy, so tasty, and kept so well?) All the way out to Coney you kept sniffing that pungent aroma of Salami and Pastrami, and by the time you got on the beach even Momma broke down and said 'All right, already; we'll eat first, but remember ... no swimming for one hour later!' "

Other early retailers on the Lower East Side scene included Schmulka Bernstein (still in wholesaling), Sussman Volk, Jacob Bronfman and Theodore Kranin.

Abe Lebewohl, owner of New York's 2nd Avenue Delicatessen-Restaurant, doesn't worry about his menus being stolen. They are offered as souvenirs. Under an ancient photo of a teeming Lower East Side street scene, the cover copy states that the menu has been prepared as "A tribute to America's greatest melting pot, and to the people who made it a significant chapter in our nation's history."

Back cover copy describes the Lower East Side in 1900 as crowded streets springing to life in a cacophony of sound. There were 25,000 pushcart peddlers in the area then. Some of their wares were tin cups, hats, eyeglasses at 35c a pair, chickens, freshly ground horseradish, suspenders, clothing, fish, roasted sweet potatoes and much, much more. People haggled loudly over prices.

"Boys and young men, bent under great mounds of half-finished garments, hurry to and from their sunless tenement flats where entire families — children, mothers, grandparents — labor from 4 a.m. to 10 at night to earn a few pennies piece-rate per garment."

Today the Lower East Side is still a bargain-hunter's paradise, and a center for avant garde art (the "East Village"). It's also "the symbol of a remarkable and fruitful era in which millions of immigrants entered the United States through one small portal, spreading across the continent and enriching the total fabric of the nation's life."

As the immigrants spread out, so did the wares purveyed by Isaac Gellis and other early provisioners. Their smoked meats were sold to groceries throughout the New York metropolitan area, and after World War I, the "appetizing delicatessen," as it was then known, appeared on the scene. The meat, fish, bread, cheese, pickles and sauerkraut already were available. All that had to be added were tables and chairs and a glass of 2¢ plain.

Mom and Pop labored long and hard in their corner deli, but they no longer prevail. Except for a fortunate few, many now simply endure. A large number closed when America's central cities closed. Some made it to the suburbs, but most could not afford shopping center rent, or were not geared for flash or glitter. Or plastic-encased pickles. Deep down in your heart, wouldn't you really rather roll up your sleeve and dig for the big one in the bottom of the barrel?

Except for the demise of the open pickle barrel (sanitation marches on), New York is the big exception, probably because it is so ungodly big. There are still some *blocks* in New York that have many more delis than some fairly large cities in the hinterlands. And you still can see salamis hanging from the rafters. That's an outlawed practice in some progressive states.

But progress marches on in other directions, too, out of Mom and Pop's hamische ambiance and into the antiseptic chrome and porcelain of the supermarket deli section.

All in the name of efficiency. That's the American way, isn't it? Listen to supermarket chain spokesmen describe the situation in their own peculiar brand of corporationese:

"Independent delis have been hit by other retailers, fast food outlets,

frozen food lines. They can't keep up (except in strong ethnic areas)
with the volume needed.

"Costs are rising fast — utilities, rent, labor and distribution — an
area in which supers tend to be efficient.

(We have) "Assured traffic space, merchandising knowledge, manufacturers' training, layout and merchandising programs ... seminars and
meetings ... manuals, on-the-job training.

"Pre-packaged cold meals would be service delis' 'hottest' items in
future years.

"We create all-inclusive box lunches ... our best seller is a ham
sandwich. It comes with Fritos, mustard and ketchup packages, salt and
a fruit." Doesn't *that* turn you on?

All is not lost, however. Hear this: Within the sterile confines of
supermarkets, their executives realize the necessity for a deli section
because of the "personal interaction and conversation," ... "personal
service and human activity in an otherwise impersonal environment."
Right on! Would you like for me maybe to open you a can sardines to
put on the Pepperidge Farm white? You want mayo, too? Sorry, that's
in Aisle 27, so schlep yourself there, but don't hit that lady with your
pushcart.

Better yet, go to Clayton, Missouri (just outside St. Louis), and meet
Bob Protzel, maybe one of the last of the Old Deli Tribe. I think I can
safely describe him as a Pop, but his beautiful young wife might
rightfully object to my including her as the other half of the Mom and
Pop team.

Nevertheless, don't ask her — or especially him — for a cold ham
sandwich and a bag of Fritos. You'll probably get hit with a herring, or
if you're really bad, with a super-dried hard salami.

Bob and Evelyn seem genuinely to enjoy doing their deli thing. He
might have his own cost-efficiency ratios, but he doesn't talk about
them. He'd rather just schmoose and hand-cut the finest lox on the west
bank of the Mississippi.

You can't just get a sandwich in his place, though. You have to listen
to him and read the signs posted behind his counter. To wit:

"We feature the leanest chicken fat in town."

"Chopped liver $7,980 per ton — may be purchased in smaller
quantities."

"Contrary to popular belief, Elmer's Glue is not a suitable substitute for anchovy paste."

"Promise her anything, but slip her a kipper."

" 'Lean' and 'diet' are four-letter words."

"Our kosher pickles made Listerine famous."

"Chopped liver and pate are the same, but pate is $1 more a
pound."

Enough signs? Listen to the man: The IRS stopped in to see him last year because he reported a rather low net income. An agent noted that he had made six trips to Europe. "Don't you see the sign?" Bob said. "We deliver!"

Before Bob bought his deli, he was in the fish business. In between he worked for a while in a butcher shop. He remembers one night when he was closing that a woman walked in and wanted a "nice chicken." He had just put the one and only chicken in the store back into the cooler, but he retrieved it, showed it to the woman, and noted that it was indeed the nicest chicken in the store; it would be a joy to her family, and she could have it for only $2.95.

She said she wanted one just a little bit bigger, so he put the chicken back, rummaged around the otherwise empty cooler, fluffed the bird's wings a little, came up with it, and said, "Aha! Here's the beauty you want. Just a little bit bigger, but gorgeous, and only $3.25."

"I can't make up my mind," she said, "the two of them look good. Wrap 'em both up."

Strange things seem to happen to Bob at closing time. People run in frantically and ask him such things as, "Could I have a half pound of corned beef for my wife?"

"No," he says. "I've seen your wife. For her I'll give you two slices salami."

Other people ask him if he carries salami. He tells them no, he just lets it lie there.

One woman came in and wanted to see his tongue. "Don't you want me to say 'ahh,' too?" he asked.

Then there was the night he was putting a huge display case of pickles to bed. A customer mused over the selection, and finally said, "I'll take that big one in the rear."

"OK, lady," Bob said. "But it's gonna smart."

Enough Protzel? No way. See his deli's listing in the guide section, or better still, go to Clayton and enjoy. You have something better to do in Missouri?

Or you could go to Mobile, Alabama and meet Mrs. Schwartz. Or Al Laks and Wally Ginsberg in Homewood, Illinois; or David Apfelbaum in San Francisco; or Sid (he wouldn't tell me his last name) in Albuquerque; or Izzy at Katz's in New York (he wouldn't tell me his last name, either), or a hundred other people, especially in New York.

The deli has evolved into a multi-ethnic national institution. Borscht is Russian; potato pancakes are German; blintzes can be Polish or French; halvah is Turkish.

American delicatessens run the ethnic gamut — Jewish, German, Hungarian, Italian, Scandinavian, Polish, Lebanese, maybe even Irish or English somewhere that I didn't find?

But I looked. Several oil company credit card departments know that I looked — they're still looking for me. My odometer racked up some

13,000 miles in THE SEARCH, plus untold miles on subways (unpleasant) and cable cars (very pleasant). Had my publisher's advances been more generous, I might have been able to say that I also employed bush pilots, helicopters, dog sleds, camel caravans and pontoon rafts. Alas, such did not occur. Assorted telephone companies increased their already exorbitant profits as I sought out distant delis in places I could not reach in person. And the U.S. Postal Service helped to some extent.

In addition to prior knowledge in some geographical areas, serendipity, suggestions by friends and bartenders, and assorted Yellow Pages, I wrote to some 100 newspaper restaurant and food writers throughout the country, asking for recommendations in their areas.

Twenty-odd came through, which advertising types tell me is a phenomenal response. However, I did make it easy for them by enclosing a self-addressed, stamped envelope. I suppose the non-respondents don't have any civic pride, or any interest in delis.

Personal contact with deli owners and managers was almost universally pleasant. Almost. But if you tell me about the one in your neighborhood that's missing from the list, it might be because nobody

would talk to me. (If I went into all of them anonymously and ate a sample of everything, I'd still be in New York, and fat.)

The biggest obstacle I had to overcome was the suspicion that I was selling something, especially advertising. (If I was selling advertising I'd be rich.) I also got the impression in a couple of places that they thought I was a revenooer. (But nobody offered me a bribe.) I did get samples, though, especially if they thought I hadn't ordered something sufficiently fattening. Sitting there stuffed, I had to listen to "Eat already; you're skinny!"

The telephone was worse. After explaining why I was calling, a not-too typical conversation might go like this:

"Why are you asking me all these questions about my store?"

"Because I'm writing a book."

"I should suffer because you're writing a book?"

"You wouldn't have to suffer. Your place will be in my book."

"What are you really selling? I don't want any."

(More explanations.)

"You're writing a book? *I* should write a book."

(Literary conversation ensues, followed by victory for hard-driving investigative deli reporter.)

"Thanks."

"OK, say what paper is this article gonna be in? I'd like to send you over a platter."

I'd like to send some platters, too — to all the newspersons who answered my plea, even those who modestly signed their missives "Anon." and especially those who sank their deli-loving teeth into the project, such as R.B. Read, author of The San Francisco Underground Gourmet and restaurant columnist for The San Francisco Examiner; Josef Mossman of the Des Moines Register and Tribune; Kenny Turan of The Washington Post, and Mike Gallagher, summer intern at the Albuquerque Journal, wherever you are now.

Also, Francee King of the Hawaii Newspaper Agency; Martha Clonis, The Youngstown Vindicator; Molly Abraham, restaurant critic of The Detroit News; Marge Hanley, food editor, The Indianapolis News; Jean Henniger, women's editor of The Oregonian, Portland: Mary K. Kilburn, "Dining Out" columnist, The Houston Chronicle; Peggy Katalinich, Taste editor of The Minneapolis Star; Delmer Robinson, Home and Family Editor, The Charleston (W. Va.) Gazette.

More platters to Abe Gellis; Al Specht of the New York deli employees union; New York PR man Mike Hall; Pickle Packers International and its kraut counterpart, both represented by Theodore R. Sills, Inc., especially Account Supervisor Saralie Slonsky; the Greatlakes Living Press co-publishing team of Keith Ray and Mike Michaelson, respectively bagel and pickle mavens, and both Chicagoland deli experts because of their gross eating habits.

Also, motel and hotel-keepers of America; their staffs, including you-know-who in Vegas; gas station operators everywhere, except the guy in Rock Springs, Wyoming who tried to rip me off (those shock absorbers are still going strong, fella); U.S. Customs and the Immigration and Naturalization Service for deigning to let me back in the country after I visited Tijuana. (Nary a deli did I find there.)

But most of all to the spiritual descendants of Isaac Gellis — delicatessen owners, managers, cooks, waiters and waitresses, countermen, busboys and cashiers (you gotta pay for what you get). And others behind the scenes — the guys who get wet while catching the fish; the cowboys who sweat while rounding up the beef; the curers and the smokers who do their sweating indoors; blessed also are the cheesemakers, the growers of kraut, and the packers of pickles; let us praise, too, the bakers of bagels and bialys and challah and rye. Where would we be without them? You'd like maybe a ham on white with a bag Fritos? Instead, enjoy.

Introducing the Perfect Nosh: The Bagel

Why do they call it a bagel?

Because it has a hole in the middle.

Why does it have a hole in the middle?

Because without the hole it wouldn't be a bagel.

You know what a bagel is, right? A bagel is "a hard roll shaped like a doughnut that is made of raised dough and cooked by simmering in water and then baked to give it a glazed brown exterior over a firm white interior," according to Mr. Webster. But what does Webster know from bagels? A bagel is an institution, not a bakery product. A bagel, to the ever-edacious deli gourmet, is the essence of American Jewish soul food. Would that it were so widely available in Israel where, according to *The Jewish Post,* the water bagel only recently was introduced on a sizeable scale (by a Russian emigre, yet!)

The perfect carrier for such comestibles as lox, cream cheese, butter and other provisions, your average bagel weighs in at about 55 grams and measures 7.62 centimeters in diameter. Perfectly delightful all by itself as a nosh or a meal, the bagel *sans* lox, cream cheese, et al is only 165 calories. It makes acceptable fare for dieters when combined with, say, only one ounce of cream cheese (about 107 calories), thus constituting a full, satisfying meal of less than 300 calories. Eat one three times a day and the bagel looks quite respectable on the menu of the weight-conscious. And, according to the U. S. Department of Agriculture, the bagel is healthful — with all of six grams of protein (two of fat), 28 grams of carbohydrate and 30 — count 'em, 30 — International (of course!) units of Vitamin A (egg bagel only; water bagels contain absolutely no Vitamin A). There also are minute amounts of other healthful substances such as calcium, iron, thiamin, riboflavin and niacin. So, if you ever needed an excuse to stuff yourself with bagels (all right already, so one is enough), there you have it.

From the beginning the bagel has been associated with happy times. According to the folks at El Al Israel Airlines, who purvey bagels as standard bill of fare and from whom much of this chapter is purloined (and thus a lift of the Leonard lid to their writer, Barbara Appel), the

bagel is a native of Vienna, born in a time of turbulence and rising (joke, get it?) to the occasion of a call to arms.

Three hundred years ago a Turkish army pillaging Vienna met an irresistible force in the minions of Polish King John Sobiesky. The hastily departing Turks left thousands of sacks of green coffee beans in their wake and an enterprising Pole, apparently well traveled and familiar with Italian coffee houses, took possession of the booty and created the first Viennese coffee house where his specialites de maison were petite half-moon shaped rolls called "kipfel." When at last the Polish liberator himself entered the city, with appreciative citizens clinging to his stirrups, our kipfel baker redesigned his bread to look like a stirrup. The word is "beugel" in German and even today there's an almost circular Austrian sweetroll bearing that name.

In time the bagel's shape rounded and after the second partition of Poland, many Jews left Austria and Germany for Galacia. The circular bread they took with them was renamed beugel, boegel or begel, depending on the region from which the baker came. After this time, the bagel immigrated to New York, but according to El Al's unidentified authority, "There is absolutely nothing original Jewish in bagels except their use at breakfast."

Until the point at which El Al took its look into the bread a few years ago, the bagel was a simple, serene bakery item of little concern to anyone except to the bagel cognoscenti whose number was thought to be so small they could hold a convention in a telephone booth. But upon publication of this capsule history, *Saturday Review* Travel Editor Horace Sutton quoted it in his column and controversy immediately engulfed the previously obscure bagel. Among many versions of the bagel's origin, as presented by *SR's* writing readers, were these:

• A Professor of Semitic Semantics argued that the square legab (left-ro-right-reading archaeologists inadvertently changed the spelling) was a favorite of the Essenes, a Jewish sect of the 2nd Century B. C. The Greek mathematician Archimedes created the legab's present perfect shape, (but square devotees still exist, for, as their current manufacturer advertises,) "A Kaufman bagel can't roll off your table."

• From ancient Egypt comes the legend of Bhagelramesis, a member of the High Court with a fondness for unsweetened doughnuts. Upon his death, he was buried according to custom, with necessities for the afterlife. When his body was exhumed recently, his doughnuts, though petrified, proved to be surprisingly edible. At least for bhagels.

• We are referred to the Biblical story of Abigail, and to the Negev desert as the real crucible of the bagel. When Abigail fled King David's amorous advances, she piled 200 loaves of dough on the backs of asses. The hot bumpy ride across the burning sands formed and baked the first Abigails, later called Bigails, now known as bagels.

• According to the authors of *Essen und Fressen,* Neanderthal man used a cementlike small ring as a weapon. When hurled at the enemy, it either (a) killed him, or (b) stunned him, or (c) so intrigued him by its aroma that he had to stop and taste it, making capture inevitable. This stone-age ring was called "the pacifier." (For current usage as such, please read on.)

• Through labyrinthian reasoning, one historian worked out the tale of Bagelus, a baker of Crete who lived in 381 B.C.E. Bagelus suffered from gout, and following the approved remedy of his time, encased his toes in warm dough and sat in the sun. One day he awoke from a nap to find his dough toe-rings baked brown and shiny, and all the animals of the neighborhood were attracted by their delectable smell. Whether Bagelus continued to make toe-ring rolls by foot or transferred his baking to the oven is not known.

• Another early Greek is said to have chided his baker for the hardness of his bread by sending him a doughnut-shaped meteoric specimen. In return the baker presented him with an unsweetened doughnut that compared favorably in firmness with the meteorite. Very little change has taken place since.

References to the bagel occur frequently in Oriental literature (if you know where to look). In this example, the bagel represents the core of ancient Chinese philosophy:

Once grasp the great form without form,
And you roam where you will
With no evil to fear,
Calm, peaceful, at ease.

The bagel's hole is in esthetic contrast to the encircling dough:

So advantage is had
From whatever is there;
But usefulness rises
From whatever is not.

(Confusing, isn't it?)

• Not all the letter writers were historians. One was an attorney, representing Mr. George F. Bagel, great-grandson of Zhellack P. Bagel, who invented the bagel in 1893. The first of Mr. Bagel's bagels were sold at the Rivington Street Bakery in New York on or about February 10, 1893, and Mr. Bagel was granted a copyright on the name in March, 1894. Fortunately, Mr. Bagel IV did not press suit.

• A more heartwarming letter came from an ex-GI, who, during action in Korea was hit three times by enemy bullets. Miraculously, each bullet struck one of the bagels his mother had sent him and which he carried in his uniform pockets. Saved his life.

The soldier is triply blessed in that the bullet missed the traditional hole in the bagel.

However, tradition probably is not the only reason for the bagel's hole. Can you imagine eating a solid bagel? It would take teeth like a crocodile's. Bakers say the hole makes the bagel easier to work with. Noshers say it gives them a better grip. Babies don't say much but those who get bagles clearly prefer them to any other teething ring. Kids like to catch the butter melting through the hole. Maybe they have the answer: the hole is for fun.

A non-bagel that does meet with the bagel set's approval is the bialy or bialystok, named after its sometimes-Russian, sometimes-Polish city of origin. Not as dashing or elegant as the bagel, the bialy slopes bumpily downward toward a center depression and its floury finish is a real hazard for diners in dark clothes. Nevertheless, its solid, bagel-type ancestry and solid, bagel chewiness make it first runner-up in lox and cream cheese circles.

But to purists, there is only one true bagel, handmade (from white wheat gluten flour, salt water, malt and yeast) and simmered in hot water for two minutes before baking. It is this simmering process, shared by the pretzel, that gives the bagel its rightful name — water bagel. A few flakes of onion or a little garlic are grudgingly permitted as signs of the times, but pumpernickel, rye, whole wheat, raisin and poppyseed varieties are merely rolls with holes — sincere forms of flattery, but not bagels.

Unfortunately for purists, most bagels today are not made by hand; the vast majority are manufactured by a machine perfected during the last decade that even makes the perfect circle that the baker's nimble fingers once created.

The bagel is becoming a cosmopolitan, even mass-merchandised, bakery product. Going, if not gone, are the basement bakeries established along New York's Lower East Side and across the bridge in Williamsburgh, Brooklyn, at the turn of the century by immigrants from Russia, Poland and the Balkans. In those days a week's wages for a bagel baker might have been two dozen bagels per day and $5 per week. As the business progressed it became almost an art and labor organizations developed as the bagel spread nationwide, now gobbling up about three cents of every $1.17 spent on bakery products.

Until comparatively recent times it was thought almost impossible to bake a bagel at home, but with a little experimentation you, too, can become a master bagel baker. Just follow this recipe:

BAGELS

2 packages dry granular yeast
4¼ to 4½ cups sifted flour
1½ cups lukewarm water
3 tablespoons sugar
1 tablespoon salt
1 egg yolk

In large bowl combine yeast and 1¾ cups flour. Combine water, sugar and salt; add to yeast mixture. Beat at low speed 30 seconds, scraping sides of bowl constantly. Beat 3 minutes at high speed. Stir in by hand enough of remaining flour to make a moderately stiff dough. Turn out on lightly floured board and knead until smooth, 5 to 8 minutes. Cover and let rest for 15 minutes.

Cut into 12 portions and shape each into smooth ball. Punch hole in center of each to resemble that of doughnut or bagel. (Alternatively, the way the pros do it: Roll the portions of dough into strips and form bagel with hand, pinching center together). Cover and let rise for 15 minutes.

Meanwhile, combine 1 gallon of water and 1 tablespoon sugar in a large kettle; bring to a boil. Reduce to simmer. Drop in 4 bagels at a time. Cook 7 minutes, turning over once. Drain on a rack. Place bagels on ungreased cookie sheet. Combine egg yolk with 2 tablespoons water. Brush each bagel with egg yolk mixture. Bake at 375 degrees for 30 to 35 minutes, or until browned.

Yield: 1 dozen   *(Bagel recipe courtesy of Chicago Tribune.)*

3 Pickles: Cucumbers with Personality

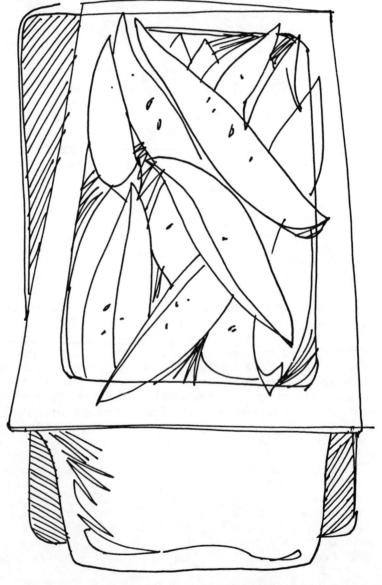

"A sandwich without a pickle is like a slap without a tickle." This uninspired piece of doggerel, plucked from a fading sign on the cluttered wall of a midtown Manhattan deli counter, nonetheless captures the spirit of the ubiquitous pickle. Thomas Jefferson, as unlikely a deli fancier as one would expect to find south of the Potomac, waxed somewhat more poetically of the captivating cucumber. "On a hot day in Virginia," he wrote, "I know of nothing more comforting than a fine spiced pickle, brought up trout-like from the sparkling depths of that aromatic jar below stairs in Aunt Sally's cellar."

Just as Aunt Sally purveyed a provocative pickle, so does Uncle Sol at the corner deli. The pickle is a delicatessen staple, as at home in the deli as a rye loaf, a knish or matzo ball soup. The fact is that the piquant condiments known collectively as pickles, including cucumbers, relishes, olives and kraut, while good by themselves, are even more esteemed for their ability to make other foods taste better. They can add sparkle and zest to a sandwich, a salad or a banquet. They can provide a change in the texture and flavor of many foods.

Through the years the perky pickle has been propagated, venerated and, compulsively it seems, alliterated. Its *aficionados* include such historical luminaries as George Washington, Cleopatra, Queen Elizabeth I and Dolly Madison, as well as a nimble-tongued pickle patron named Peter Piper and a contemporary character with the improbable name of Pickerman the Pickle Packer (about whom more later). But while it seems easy to take the pickle to the platter, it apparently is difficult to take it seriously. Pyjamaed and raincoated husbands of pickle-craving mothers-to-be still pop up in the tired plots of television sitcoms. Those same husbands sooner or later find cause to become pickled imbibers who either en route or upon reaching home find themselves in a terrible and frequently unfunny pickle. Even the staid Pickle Packers International, Inc., has difficulty in taking its product seriously. In corresponding about this book, the PPI declared that our interest in "Thinking Pickles" had caused them to be "Pickled Tink" (honest, they did).

Despite this propensity for playful puns (you see, it is compulsive), the pickle is big business and growing bigger. The United States population now consumes close to 18 billion pounds per year (more than double the consumption of 20 years ago), a rate equal to 8.3 pounds per capita. Annual retail sales of pickles now exceed $500 million. Not bad for a sour-faced green vegetable with warts.

Pickling — as a means of preserving food — is of ancient lineage, along with sun-drying, salting and smoking. Perhaps it all started centuries ago when a naturally bitter olive fell into a briny lagoon and was found to be edible, tasty and nourishing. Be that as it may, the art of pickling can be traced through thousands of years of recorded history — and beyond.

The pickle is as old as antiquity. People were eating pickles before civilizations kept written records. In approximately 2030 B.C. inhabitants of northern India brought the seeds of the cucumber to the Tigris Valley where preservation of fruits and vegetables soon became common practice. The use of the pickle quickly spread throughout European and

Western cultures. During the 17th Century, pickles appeared in the colonies, and in 1820, the first pickle-packing plant came into being. Pickles, now past their 4000th year, are produced in 39 states with Michigan in first place for total production.

Michigan also is the home of one Pickerman the Pickle Packer to whom we referred earlier. Pickerman — alias Len Dennison, a former deli owner of Ann Arbor — first came to official notice when he telephoned the department of weights and measures at the Ann Arbor city hall.

"This is Pickerman the pickle packer," he announced. "I am opening a pickle store and want to get my scale certified."

Seconds later, when he called back, he was able to convince the incredulous clerk that he was for real. The bureau sent out an inspector in about 10 minutes.

Pickerman — Len Dennison — for many years had the idea of opening a store devoted to purveying the ever-popular pickle. He realized his dream in May, 1976, when he opened a store in the Kerrytown Market, an indoor mall adjacent to a popular Ann Arbor farmer's market at 407 North Fifth Avenue.

Pickle champions will find that the shopping mall is a friendly sort of place whose customers include students and professors' wives, hailing from all areas of Ann Arbor. There's usually lots of kidding at the Pickerman booth, Len Dennison enjoying banter with customers as he cuts up chunks of pickles for sampling. "They laughed when I sat down to think up a pickle store," says Dennison. Now, with the Ann Arbor operation dispensing 100 gallons of pickles on a busy Saturday, there are two more Pickerman Pickle Packer stores on the drawing boards — at Birmingham, Michigan and in Ohio — and there is some talk of a franchise.

Operating from a booth decorated with timber from a 100-year-old barn (Pickerman's floor is the actual floor from the barn's hayloft), Pickerman carries a variety of pickles, kraut, peppers, pickled tomatoes, Greek olives, black olives, stuffed eggplant, grape leaves, bulk mustard, marinated egg plant and gardinere, a mixture of pickled cauliflower and other vegetables. A refrigerator case carries New York cheese cake, salads, knishes and other deli goodies.

Pickles are dispensed from barrels and include kosher dills, fresh-processed dills, German pickles, sweet gherkins and New England sour gherkins. Other pickled stuff includes pickled green tomatoes, hot finger peppers, hot cherry peppers, sweet red bell peppers and sweet yellow peppers. Enhancing Pickerman's continental flavor is a German-style kraut made with bacon, juniper berries and cornichons, a French variety of the pickle. Biggest pickle sellers so far are kosher dills and fresh packed dills running neck to neck, says Dennison, with weight watchers prefering the latter because they absorb less salt. Bagels are another popular item at Pickerman, with 100 dozen sold in five hours during a recent Saturday.

Through the years, many famous persons have not only expressed a fondness for the condiment but have claimed health benefits as well from pickle-popping. Cleopatra is said to have believed pickles contributed to health and beauty and Napoleon esteemed pickles as a health-giving food. Today's weight-conscious pickle fanciers can take comfort in the fact that a large dill pickle contains only 11 calories. (The nutritive value of four popular pickle types is detailed in the accompanying chart.)

Historically, the pickle patch was an important adjunct to good living on colonial plantations. And pickles were highly regarded by pioneering generations because, under frontier conditions, pickles were the only zestful and succulent food available for many months of the year. In colonial days, and much later on the farms and in the villages, homemakers expected to "put down" some pickles in stone crocks — and to "put up" pickles and pickle relishes in glass jars.

Pickles are a product of natural fermentation — either of the vegetable or food ingredients or of the liquid surrounding them. This fermentation process, carefully controlled by the amount of salt used, the temperature, herbs, spices and other factors, develops the flavor, color, aroma and texture desired for the particular kind of pickle.

Soil, rainfall and location all have a decisive effect on growth of just the right kind of tender, flavorful cucumber for pickling. Agriculturalists and scientists have supplied growers with improved varieties and advised farmers as to the best methods of planting and cultivating in order to produce firmer, meatier cucumbers.

Cucumbers are picked at a time when most of them are of the sizes particularly wanted by the packer. The bulk of this work has been done by hand. In the larger "pickle patches" of today, a strong trend is toward mechanically harvesting the cucumbers very quickly at the peak of their quality.

Since most pickles are cucumber pickles or contain cucumber pickles in a mixture, we will concentrate mostly on them. Because of the way they are made they are called either "cured pickles" or "fresh pack pickles." Each has its own characteristics of flavor and texture.

Cured pickles have been slightly fermented in a salt brine for several months. They are then de-salted and washed. The pickling process is completed in a vinegar solution, also a fermentation product, and seasoned to give the flavor characteristics desired. The curing process imparts subtle flavor changes and produces edible acids in the pickles themselves. They are usually crisp, dark green and somewhat translucent.

Fresh-packed pickles are relatively new. In this process the cucumbers are packed directly into the containers and covered with a pickling solution containing vinegars, other acids, flavorings and other suitable ingredients to give the desired characteristics to the pickles. The containers are then sealed and pasteurized with heat to preserve them. Fresh-pack pickles have not been fermented and retain something of the flavor of fresh cucumbers. They are usually a light yellow-green color and are not as salty or as acid as the cured type. "Fresh-pack" is often shown on the label.

In modern-day pickling, cucumbers to be cured are hauled to salting stations close to the growing regions. The newly harvested cucumbers go there for a thorough cleansing and careful sorting for defects and sizes. Speed is essential while the cucumbers are at their peak of perfection, and it is provided by efficient, modern machinery.

For cured pickles, the selected cucumbers are put in a salt water bath in vats, where controlled fermentation takes place. The salt is added gradually, according to an exact formula, and it penetrates the pickles slowly, evenly and thoroughly.

After weeks and even months of such curing, the cucumbers are

called "brine stock." The brine stock may then be removed from the salting station to the finishing plant, according to the plant's schedule. Cucumbers for fresh pack are hauled directly to the packing plant since they must be processed within a few hours.

The kinds of pickles for sale are almost as infinite as the kinds of cooking that exist. While the number of different styles, colors and shapes that fill the shelves can be confusing, all cucumber pickles are related to one or another of a simple handful of basic varieties. Here are some typical variations.

The following data on typical varieties will steer you to the perfect pickle every time.

Dill Pickles

Dill pickles are flavored primarily with dill, an aromatic herb, that may be supplemented by various mixed spices. They come in three variations. Genuine dill pickles are prepared entirely by a lengthy process of natural fermentation with the various herbs. Processed dill pickles are started as regular brine stock and finished later in a dill solution; they possess somewhat better keeping qualities than the genuine dill pickles. Between these falls an occasional "overnight dill" pickle. This is a quickly fermented variation of the genuine dill pickle produced by stopping the fermentation after only a day or two by placing the pickles in cold storage. These pickles retain some of the flavor of the fresh cucumber, along with the dill flavor. Like the genuine dills, they are commonly sold in bulk.

The label may indicate that many of these dills are "kosher" or "kosher-style" pickles. While, of course, the term "kosher" has religious significance in accord with Jewish law, in the United States it also has come to mean that these pickles are more highly spiced, including onion and garlic flavors.

Most dill pickles are large or medium in size. They may have been cut into strips, slices, cubes or any other shape.

Sour Pickles

These are brine stock pickles that have been finished in vinegar with spices. While normally packed whole, they may be cut into strips, slices or other forms. There are a number of different styles, such as sour mixed pickles — produced by combining sour cucumber pickles with other sour pickled vegetables such as cauliflower, onions, peppers, all cut into small convenient pieces. Sour relish or piccalilli includes finely chopped sour pickles, sometimes packed alone and sometimes with other finely chopped sour-cured vegetables. Chow chow is similar to sour mixed pickles except for the addition of a mustard sauce flavored with spices such as yellow and brown mustard seed, turmeric, garlic, cinnamon, cloves, ginger, nutmeg, cayenne and black and white pepper.

Sweet Pickles

These are sour pickles from which the vinegar has been drained. They are finished in sweet, spicy liquors that are added from time to time until the desired degree of sweetness is attained. A lengthy aging process follows. Sweet pickles are available in many variations: sliced sweet pickles, chips or wafers, plain sweet pickles cut crosswise into discs; candied chips — extra sweet, sliced sweet pickles; sweet dill pickles — made from genuine or processed dill pickles instead of sour pickles and frequently cut lengthwise as well as crosswise; mixed sweet pickles — sweet pickles combined with other sweet pickled vegetables, such as cauliflower, onions, sweet pepper, and green tomatoes; sweet relish or piccalilli — finely chopped sweet pickles sometimes combined with other finely chopped sweet pickled vegetables.

Some of the pickles that are classified as cured type are also available in the fresh pack type. Among them are fresh-packed dill pickles, fresh-packed sweet pickles and mild sweet pickles, fresh-packed sweet relish and mild sweet relish, fresh-packed sweetened dill pickles and fresh-packed sweetened dill relish.

Pickles belong to a larger family of foods with many of the same characteristics, adding interest and zest to your meals. Many other fruits and vegetables are pickled commercially or by homemakers. Some often seen on the store shelf are peach, pear, crabapple, watermelon rind, beet, onion, okra, peppers, tomatoes — ripe or green — and green beans.

Also available are a variety of old-fashioned, unusual relishes, such as pepper-onion, tomato apple-chutney, tomato-pear chutney, horseradish and corn relish.

Sauerkraut also belongs in this large family of foods. Good sauerkraut — brined, fermented cabbage — has a pleasant, characteristic, tart and tangy flavor. It is crisp and firm in texture, creamy white in color and free from specks and core material. It is used hot in many ways — as a main dish with meat, or in most of the ways pickles are used, cold as a side dish, in sandwiches, on a salad plate or in a mixed pickle and relish platter.

Cured olives also belong in this family since they are used in much the same manner. Serve them the way you would cucumber pickles — whole or chopped, sliced or stuffed.

As with many other available foods, pickles and relishes are packed quite often according to U.S. grades. These grades, with their definitions of styles, forms and kinds, help manufacturers make and label the products they offer for sale. U.S. grades also help the store buyers stock what the consumers want.

Here are some tips on what to look for in a pickle purchase:

• First look at the whole pickle display — including the product as seen through the glass container. You can usually tell whether the cucumbers are whole, sliced crosswise, sliced lenthwise, unevenly cut or finely cut as in a relish. You can also choose the size you want. Cucumber pickles come in seven regular sizes from the midget to the extra large. You can

often examine the jars of mixed pickles and relishes to see what
ingredients are used and in what proportions.
• Read the labels; they give much useful information. For one thing,
labels may suggest kinds and styles you have never encountered. Information on the label that can help in your selection includes the kind of
pickles — sweet, sour or dill; the size or number in the container;
whether they are the cured or fresh type; and the amount of product in
the container.
• Note the prices asked; they vary considerably from item to item and
from brand to brand. This is often because some types are much more
costly to make. Small whole cucumbers, long processes, and more costly
spices and other ingredients are reasons for higher priced items. They
may well be worth the higher price for some purposes. Small whole
cucumber pickles would not be a good buy, however, if you intend to
slice them into a salad or a sandwich.

• Buy different kinds to add variety to your meals and to learn what your family really likes.

Pickles can be perfect partners, enhancing other foods, especially leftovers, such as meat loaf, hash or less expensive cuts of meat. The potential of pickles as snacks or appetizers is tremendous. Crackers with various spreads topped with stuffed pickle slices are delicious. Small hors d'oeuvres kebobs made with pickles, shrimp, cherry tomatoes, etc., have eye as well as appetite appeal. Prepared dishes take on a "dressed-up" look when garnished with pickles; fish, blended salads (potato salad, macaroni salad, etc.), sandwiches, roasts and casseroles.

Pickles also function notably as a main dish ingredient such as in sweet and sour pork or Creole dishes. Diced pickles may be added to stuffings, meat, fish or vegetable salads. Pickle chips blend well with creamed or buttered vegetables. Many kinds of sauces for meats, fish, fowl or egg dishes contain pickles. The following are some additional suggestions for using pickles and relishes:

• In the lunchbox alone or in the sandwich mix.
• A sprinkle of chopped pickle or relish in almost any soup.
• Diced in stuffings, meat loaves or meat dishes, fish, salads, creamed or buttered vegetables.
• Diced pickles, olives or relishes in scrambled eggs.
• Pickles or their liquids in sauces for meats, fish, fowl, egg dishes.
• The liquid from pickles in almost any dressing or to baste the meat.
• Wherever a bit of spice or herb flavor is needed.

You can keep pickles and relishes unopened for several months. After opening, store them in the refrigerator. Natural acids in the food and the surrounding liquor tend to inhibit the growth of molds and bacteria.

Pickles and relishes will not keep for an indefinite period, however. Discard any open jar if the product is very discolored, if it has an offensive odor, if gas bubbles appear, or if the product displays any unusual softness, mushiness or slipperiness.

NUTRITIVE VALUE OF PICKLES

The data listed below show the nutritive value of 100 grams of pickle, approximately one large dill or one-half cup of fresh cucumber pickle slices.

	Genuine Dill Pickles		Sweet Pickles		Sour Pickles		Fresh Pack Cucumber Pickles	
Water	93.3%		60.7%		94.8%		78.7%	
Food Energy ...	11	calories	146	calories	10	calories	73	calories
Protein	.7	gm.	.7	gm.	.5	gm.	0.9	gm.
Fat	.2	gm.	.4	gm.	.2	gm.	.2	gm.
Carbohydrate ..	2.2	gms.	36.5	gms.	2.0	gms.	17.9	gms.
Ash	3.6	gms.	1.7	gms.	2.5	gms.	2.3	gms.
Calcium	26.0	mgs.	12.0	mgs.	17.0	mgs.	32.0	mgs.
Iron	1.0	mg.	1.2	mgs.	3.2	mgs.	1.8	mgs.
Vit. A	100	I.U.	90	I.U.	100	I.U.	140	I.U.
Thiamine		trace		trace		trace		trace
Riboflavin	.02	mg.	.02	mg.	.02	mg.	.03	mg.
Vit. C	6.0	mgs.	6.0	mgs.	7.0	mgs.	9.0	mgs.
Phosphorus	21.0	mgs.	16.0	mgs.	15.0	mgs.	27.0	mgs.
Potassium	200.0	mgs.	–		–		–	
Sodium	1428.0	mgs.	–		1353.0	mgs.	673.0	mgs.

Research at Michigan State College showed that the Vitamin A content of cucumbers is increased during the pickling process; Vitamin C decreased. The less highly processed pickle types, the pasteurized dills and fresh cucumber pickles, using pickles processed by fresh-pack method from cucumbers maintain more of the Vitamin C content of the fresh cucumber.

If you still can't seem to find a pickle to suit your personality, consult the chart below for astrological guidance.

Sign	Personality	Birth	Pickle
Pisces	sweet, tender	2/20 – 3/20	Sweet Gherkins
Aries	fiery, inquisitive	3/20 – 4/19	Hot Mixed Pickles
Taurus	dependable, basic	4/20 – 5/20	Dill Hamburger Slices
Gemini	likes variety	5/21 – 6/21	Sweet Mixed Pickles
Cancer	hospitable, loves garnishes	6/22 – 7/21	Kosher Dill Spears
Leo	dramatic, personable	7/22 – 8/21	Hot Dog Relish
Virgo	gentle, a good moneymaker	8/22 – 9/22	Midget Gherkins
Libra	diplomatic, lover of beauty	9/23 – 10/22	Sweet Fresh Cucumber Pickles
Scorpio	definite opinions, passionate	10/23 – 11/21	Sliced Sour Pickles
Sagittarius	friendly, enjoys outdoors	11/22 – 12/21	Hamburger Relish
Capricorn	mild tempered, industrious	12/22 – 1/20	Polish-style Dill Pickle Spears
Aquarius	independent, generous	1/21 – 2/19	Candied Sweet Pickle Chips

4 Something Fishy at the Deli

Fish, deli-style, has two distinguishing characteristics. It usually is served cold; it often is smoked. It also can be exceedingly expensive – witness the $12-15 per pound currently being asked for Nova Scotia lox (prime smoked salmon). Or it can be a gastronomic bargain. At Langer's deli in Los Angeles, for instance, an appetizer of pickled or schmaltz herring with a serving of bread and butter is proffered for $1.55.

Fish from a deli also can provide a delightfully uncomplicated meal – or it can form the basis of an elegant repast. What could be more simple, or savory, than a Sunday breakfast of lox, bagels and cream cheese served with all the news that is fit to print? On the other hand, food critic/author James Beard writes of friends who are noted for the gracious style in which they entertain on Sunday mornings in their handsome New York apartment. In *James Beard's Fish Cookery*, the author describes those Sunday brunches at his friends' apartment. The meal centers around an imposing oval table, the cynosure of which is a large, tempting platter of smoked whitefish, smoked salmon and smoked sturgeon with thinly sliced Bermuda onion and lemon wedges. Then comes a steaming dish of fluffy scrambled eggs accompanied by hot rolls. "This is," notes Beard, "a superb combination of flavors."

Variety also is a surprising characteristic of deli fish dishes, which can include herring, salmon, sturgeon, cod, carp and whitefish in addition to the prosaic likes of canned tuna and sardines and that ubiquitous Jewish hybrid, gefilte fish. For example, within the heterogeneous ranks of herring are specimens that are pickled, kippered and creamed. Other herring appear in marinades of wine or, as it is served at David's in San Francisco, in a sour cream sauce. Others, if they have a proclivity to plumpness, may find themselves described on a deli menu as schmaltz, matjas or maatjes. Herring also may be found swimming (figuratively, we trust) in tomato sauce, oil or vinegar. In the latter instance, they may be known as Bismarck herring or, if they are pickled, rolled and speared with toothpicks, as rollmops. If a herring shows up that is colored a reddish, dark brown, it has been cured by heavy salting and slow smoking and is ideally suited, both literally and figuratively, for drawing across the trail of a fox to mask the scent and confound the hunting dogs.

Kippered herring — the "kipper" of the classic British breakfast dish — showed up in some of the delis we visited in the course of preparing this book. Canter's of Los Angeles offers fried kippered herring as an entree, while New York's Ratner's suggests broiled kippered herring with potato and onion. A kipper is a herring that has been split open, gutted, soaked in brine and smoked using oak chips and sawdust. Kippers also lend themselves to poaching and are simply ambrosial when brushed with butter and lemon, seasoned with paprika and baked in an oiled, shallow dish. Scrambled eggs make a good companion to this savory, smoky breakfast or luncheon dish.

Actually, the versatile herring is a flavorful and eminently nutritious fish in abundant supply that for centuries has been regarded as a valuable food source. Certainly, little is wasted. Fish too small to market as herrings are popped into cans and sold as sardines. The roe of the fish

can be mixed with chopped eggs to make lively hors d'oeuvres; the milt can be beaten into herring sauces and marinades. Even the scales of herrings have been utilized to make imitation mother of pearl shirt buttons.

Generally speaking, herring, along with such other deli fish favorites as canned salmon, sardines and tuna, can be classed as a fat, rather than a lean, fish. A herring has approximately 12.5 percent fat (based on the composition of raw flesh) — compared to 1.3 percent for turbot and a mere 0.6 percent for cod. On the other hand, herring contains close to 200 calories per 100-gram serving compared to a svelte-suggesting 60 calories per 100 grams of cod and only 43 calories in a like serving of turbot.

Calorie-counting, however, surely is as incongruous in a deli as a pastrycook on a fat farm. More in character is the colorful humor of our friend, St. Louis deli owner Bob Protzel, who shares with us some amusing insights into the selection of a herring:

"Buying a schmaltz herring," he observes, "requires a particular skill which cannot be acquired by anyone but a typical Jewish housewife. Anyone can select a ripe watermelon. All that is needed is an educated thumb and index finger. If you want to know whether an ear of corn is desirable, just strip down the husk when the storekeeper isn't looking. A gentle squeeze is all it takes to test the firmness of a tomato. If you aren't sure how long a bag of potato chips has been on the shelf, just crush it and listen for a crisp response.

"It's different, however, with a herring. Perhaps 'knowledge' is a better word than 'skill' to describe what is needed to select one. For instance, all herrings look alike. Any family characteristics that a herring might possess are immediately lost when the head is lopped off for packing. Even the sex of a herring is indistinguishable, unless it is found to contain either milt or roe, which determines gender — if you happen to recognize milt or roe when you see them. I don't.

"So, now that we have established the fact that herrings are identical, from the standpoint of appearance, it naturally follows (in the analytical mind of an old-fashioned herring pickler,) that if one herring is more desirable than another, the most sought-after must be the one most difficult to get at. Hence, all good herrings are reputedly at the bottom of the barrel.

"Eating a herring from the top of the barrel is almost as sacrilegious to the average Jewish diner as sharing a pork roast with an Arab. But there's the rub. When you consider that the gross profit (five cents, average) realized from the sale of a barrel-bottom herring is the same as that from a topside herring, and carries with it the necessity of a 15-minute scrub-down of hands, wrists, elbows and fingernails with a wire brush and scouring powder, it isn't difficult to understand why most deli operators are 'sold out' whenever they get a request for a

herring during a busy time of the day."

Although it is rare today to find a deli that is strictly kosher, observing without deviation the traditional Jewish ritual and dietary laws (in fact, many modern delis cannot be characterized as Jewish and many others, of course, owe their ethnic loyalties to other races and creeds,) it is helpful to the perspective of this book to note the few kosher rules that govern the use of fish. You won't find an eel in a strictly kosher kitchen (nor in any deli we encountered in researching this book) since fish that do not have scales are taboo – *trefe* or *trefah* as these prohibited foods are called. Thus shellfish and crustaceans also are eschewed under the Rules of Kashruth. This, of course, eliminates such goy gustatory gratifications as lobster, crab, clams, oysters and shrimp. As a matter of fact, while the state of Israel does have a shrimp fishery, it is geared to the export market.

There has been speculation that ancient scholars formulated many of the kosher dietary laws as sound sanitary practices. Pork, for example, even with modern sanitary controls, can carry virulent trichinosis. Shellfish, unlike fish that have "fins and scales," tend to remain in relatively small areas and thus could be more susceptible to contamination. Modern outbreaks of hepatitis have been traced to contaminated oyster beds.

Nothing could be farther removed from the homebody oyster than the peripatetic salmon, which has migrating instincts and a strength that enables it to cover upward of 75 miles a day and travel as much as 200 miles inland from the ocean. Internationally regarded as a gourmet item, the salmon lends itself to baking, broiling, poaching, frying, canning and potting. It is, however, the processes of smoking, salting and kippering that most immediately interest deli devotees.

Epicureans regard Scottish smoked salmon as tops, followed by Norwegian and then Canadian — specifically, that which originates from the maritime provinces and which is known as Nova Scotia or simply Nova salmon. This latter type appears on many deli menus along with the more salty lox (the Russian word for salmon). In addition to cream cheese and bagels, compatible accompaniments for this fish include capers, course black pepper, sliced onion, lemon wedges, sliced eggs and scrambled eggs, along with rye, pumpernickel or thin slices of buttered wholewheat bread — and a parsley or watercress garnish. Many delis team lox with onions and/or scrambled eggs. In New York, the Stage deli offers "The Twosome" (for two people, the menu explains redundantly) consisting of three bagels, Nova Scotia salmon, cream cheese and lake sturgeon. Also in Gotham, Ratner's serves a unique pickled lox.

Kippered salmon, found at some delis, is a fine breakfast dish, or great for lunch with a salad. At Canter's of Los Angeles, kippered salmon is offered as a breakfast entree accompanied by onion and tomato. Simply, kippered salmon is fish that has been cooked during the smoking process.

Even though many latterday delis and many of the items they sell are losing their identity in our increasingly homogeneous society, there remains at least one popular deli fish entree that retains its distinct ethnic character. Gelfilte fish (also known as gefuelte or gefeullte), popular in many of the delicatessens visited during the writing of this book, remains undeniably Jewish. In fact, gefilte (from the German for "stuffed" or "filled") is a traditional first course of Sabbath eve meals and is a popular dish during Jewish holidays.

There are many variations to gefilte fish. It can be served hot or cold. Langer's deli in Los Angeles offers it both ways; David's of San Francisco serves gefilte appetizers with matzo or chale (egg twist). Traditionally, in preparing gefilte, the filleted meat of the fish is chopped and returned to the fish between skin and backbone. Modern variations produce patties made from ground fish (carp, pike, whitefish and buffalo commonly are used either singly or in combination). Onions, eggs, bread or matzo, seasonings and perhaps diced celery and carrots also go

into these fish balls. Cooked carrot slices and horseradish (colored and flavored with beet juice) are customary accompaniments.

Some historians indicate that this dish may have originated in Russia or Poland, where it was known as Jewish fish; others trace its possible origins to Holland or Germany following the expulsion of Spain's Jewish community in 1492. Whatever its true origin, the dish remains a popular one on Jewish tables around the world and among the Jewish and Gentile patrons of many of America's delis.

Gefilte fish can be an excellent low-budget, protein-rich dish for the family table, a means of grinding up and using leftover fish — a sort of aquatic meat loaf. At the other end of the budgetary scale, splurging deli fans may want to try the party trays from Fine and Schapiro's (138 W. 72nd Street, New York). These include miniature fish balls and a lavish fish canape platter that includes black and red caviar, anchovies and herring. At those prices, we hope the herring are from the bottom of the barrel.

Stalking
the Elusive Deli

5

Once upon a time, on a crisp Midsummer Midwestern morning, I headed south from Chicago toward New Orleans. I didn't get there until the following day, but meanwhile, I traversed southern Illinois, a little piece of Missouri's bootheel, *ein bissel* Arkansas, likewise a little bit of Tennessee, and came to a roaring halt in Jackson, Mississippi.

Early on that Midsummer Morn, I tried to check out Bubby and Zadie's Deli in Champaign, but it didn't open until 11:30, so I went across the street and had an Egg McMuffin at the campus McDonald's. (Lest effete easterners wonder whereof I speak, Champaign-Urbana is the seat of Illinois' higher educational system, where Illini teams are wont to lose a lot.)

Which is why the immediately following narrative opens in New Orleans, proceeds across the Gulf Coast to Mobile, and then goes north and west through Mississippi, another part of Louisiana, into Texas, onward and upward through the Rockies and the deserts unto the Promised Land of California. (With a very short side trip to Tijuana.)

Combined with the return trip from California, primarily via Interstate 80, this was the longest leg of the Deli Odyssey. (It was preceded by a couple of eastern ventures, which always ended at Charlie Brown's in the Pan Am building.)

The publisher assures me that alphabetical cross-references will be made, so that you can check out your favorites in your favorite state. (Sorry, Alaska et al., you just didn't respond.)

On this recent Southern stalk of the elusive deli, I did not go from Natchez to Mobile, but I did go from Mobile to Natchez. (If anybody cares, I also did not go from Memphis to St. Joe.)

En route from Mobile to Natchez, my Maverick carried me to Hattiesburg sometime between lunch and the cocktail hour. I stopped at the local branch of a very prominent overpriced roadside inn, checked the Yellow Pages, found there were no delis listed, went to the john and repaired to the bar where I ordered a Coke (with lime). The rather bosomy barmaid seemed a bit miffed that I did not wany any booze in

my Coke. Nevertheless, I stuck to my longtime no-drinkee-while-driving resolve even though the barmaid's equally bosomy buddy muttered what might be described as an epithet and moved several stools away. How did they know I was a Yankee liberal and maybe even a *prevert?*

I got the hell out of there, assuming that a lynching was less possible in the 100-degree parking lot, and checked my trusty Rand-McNally Atlas. Though there was a somewhat more direct route to Natchez, I decided to go through Collins, Mississippi, because I was in the Army with a guy from Collins.

Collins turned out to be a veritable metropolis. There was a gas station for which I had a credit card, and it *is* the county seat of Covington County. Also, I became a bit of a short-term celebrity. It turned out that my Army buddy was one of the town's leading citizens. He's still in the Army. In Germany.

Seriously, though, I like Collins, even though it doesn't have a deli. The gas station owner suggested that I might like to move down there and go into the lumbering business. It didn't seem like a bad idea, however impractical, but instead I lumbered off toward Natchez.

A road sign, and the atlas, tempted me toward nearby Hot Coffee, Mississippi, but the heat and my resolve to make Natchez by nightfall were enough to shake off the temptation. Hell, if I'd gone there, the map also beckoned toward Lake Como and Heidelberg, Mississippi. Who knows what that would have led to — Stonewall, Increase, Enterprise, Energy, Hurricane Creek or Whynot? Earlier in the day I had similarly resisted a side trip to Brooklyn, even though I was born in *the* Brooklyn.

Anyway, I got to Natchez and bedded down after devouring some succulent New Orleans oysters at what appeared to be Natchez's leading motel's restaurant. (No delis, but I couldn't believe the accent of the Big Daddy type at the next table. Move over, Orson Welles.)

As Spiro might have said, when you've seen one ante-bellum home, you've seen them all, so the next morning I crossed some river into Louisiana. I went through Waterproof and Alligator Bayou and stopped for breakfast in Monroe.

No delis, so I stopped in the local drugstore and watched the cook attempt to crack an egg. After a half hour or so my caffeine craving became so bad that I went across the street to the five-and-dime.

Immediate service. Fantastic. I struck up a conversation with my next-stool companion, who seemed pretty safe since she was a police-woman. She confirmed what I had already perceived — no delis, but a great desire on the part of the people for what they have to offer. The South may be the Last Frontier for a smart young Yankee with chutzpah, some gelt and a slab of redolent lox. (It also wouldn't hurt if he knew how to make a bagel.)

French Market Grocery
839 Decatur St.
New Orleans   581-9347

The French Market Grocery in New Orleans (839 Decatur Street) might qualify as a traditional deli only because corned beef and pastrami are available in the winter.

However, don't miss the muffuletta — New Orleans' equivalent of bagels and lox, corned beef and swiss, or whatever the epitome of delicatessenhood may be.

This Creole-Italian creation is a comestible conglomerate that features such internationally oriented goodies as provolone, salami and other assorted Italian coldcuts, Italian or Polish ham, topped with a home-made secret-recipe type olive salad. Better bring some friends along to help you eat it, because it's served on an eight-to-ten-inch-diameter sesame muffuletta loaf.

The ubiquitous New Orleans Poor Boys also are available, as are shrimp and oyster loaf. Naturally, the French Market Grocery carries a complete line of groceries — domestic, imported, and New Orleans specialties, including coffees, crab boil, Creole mustard, gumbo *file,* spicy pickled onions, soups, and crawfish *etouffee.* Boiled seafood is featured on weekends.

Take-out or send-out (catalog available), the French Market Grocery is open 9 a.m. to 7 p.m., seven days a week. 581-9347.

Central Grocery
923 Decatur St.
New Orleans   523-1620

Down the street at 923 Decatur is the Central Grocery, "Home of the Original Muffuletta." My cryptic notes tell me it "smells good — in old barracks."

The cool and spicy aroma that hits you when you walk in out of the semi-tropical sun is not what you'd expect in a barracks, however. Probably because it was a barracks a couple of hundred years ago.

The Central Grocery carries a complete imported and domestic line. In addition to carry-outs it does a mail order business. 523-1620.

Cafe Maspero
440 Rue Chartres
New Orleans   523-8414

Gilded signs on New Orleans' Cafe Maspero proclaim, "Since 1788." Back then, though, it was Pierre Maspero's Slave Exchange.

Today's cafe is located at 440 Rue Chartres, at the corner of Rue St. Louis in the French Quarter. Among the menu features are char-broiled burgers with and without cheese and/or chili, ham, corned beef, a combination cheese board, and the best-seller — pastrami with imported cheese.

You can also have the homemade chili without a burger, or a rib eye steak sandwich. Fries also available. French, of course.

There's an extensive wine list, and it's available by the glass, carafe, liter, bottle and half bottle. Beer, booze, and all kinds of cocktails can be had — including New Orleans exotics such as Hurricanes, Planters Punch, Zombies, Ramos Gin Fizz, and peach, banana, lime, strawberry and pineapple daiquiris. Tables are arranged outdoor cafe-style indoors on a gleaming tile floor; there are take-outs, and you can eat at the bar if your mother told you to keep your elbows off the table.

Open 11-12, seven days a week. 523-8414.

Serio's Delicatessen and Po-Boys
130 St. Charles St.
New Orleans   523-2668

Just across Canal Street from the French Quarter, at 130 St. Charles Street, is Serio's Delicatessen and Po-Boys, an interesting mix of Italian, kosher, and New Orleans cuisines.

Serio's has a good variety of standard deli meats, plus homemade Italian olives and salads, muffulettas, meatballs, and Po Boys.

Manager Jack Serio introduced this Yankee to the classic New Orleans roast beef Po Boy — beef, lettuce, and mayonnaise drenched with gravy. (The natives like a lot of gravy.) Thank you, Jack.

Serio's is for day people — open from 6:30 a.m. 'til 4:30 p.m. six days a week. As they say in the Crescent City, it's dark on Sunday. 523-2668.

Schwartz Kosher Market and Delicatessen
53 S. Georgia Ave.
Mobile   432-0891

You've heard of Mobile, Alabama, right? But have you ever heard of a Jewish oasis in the middle of all those azaleas? So believe, there is one. Stop by 53 South Georgia Avenue and meet Mrs. Schwartz.

She holds forth at the Schwartz Kosher Market and Delicatessen, in a place where you wouldn't expect her — or it — to be.

There are only a couple of tables, and if you inhale, you might think you're back in New York. Also, if you look at her with the eyes that God gave you, you might think the same thing.

Listen, too. What is she saying? What's for sale? What's for sale is kosher — in Mobile! It includes homemade blintzes, knishes, kreplach and other deli dishes . . . in Mobile!

Mrs. Schwartz is a beautiful lady ... When I first met her she thought maybe I was selling advertising or something, but when I convinced her I was only writing a book, she bought me an iced tea. That was very welcome, because it was August in Mobile and it was very, very hot. However, I thought that if it was winter in Mobile (if there is such a season there) she would have insisted that I drink my chicken soup.

It has been said by the prophets or somebody that everybody has a namesake, or a face-sake, or a body-sake. If this is true, Golda Meir, listen — before you retire to the Negev (and I hope you never do), first come to Mobile and meet your spiritual sister Mrs. Schwartz. She's there from 9 a.m. to 5 p.m., Monday through Friday. Call her at 432-0891.

Grapes Unlimited, Inc.
301 Government St.
Mobile   433-2333

Also in Mobile, Manuel X. Green runs Grapes Unlimited, Inc., at 301

Government Street in the east wing of the Sheraton Inn.

It's a deli — sort of — but in a very limited space. Manuel, who's been in business only a little less than a year, is proud of the fact that his is the first such hotel shop in Alabama.

He has a good selection of wine (hence the name), kosher and Danish salami, domestic and imported cheeses, lots of canned goods, plus beer and soft drinks.

If you're too bedraggled after fighting the Alabama sun to face the Sheraton's dining room, you can find plenty to nosh on at Grapes. Take it upstairs, kick off your shoes and enjoy.

Y'all come on downstairs later and send some postcards home to the folks. They're available at Grapes, as are other souvenirs.

If you're traveling with your secretary, or don't feel guilty and yet munificent, check Manuel's turquoise and silver jewelry. It's one of the best-looking selections I've seen that side of Albuquerque, but don't pin me down on prices or authenticity, please. I shop for my daughters among members of the Taiwan tribe in San Francisco.

Lest Jorgen Hansen of Hilton and my friends in other caravanseries feel that I have implied that one must be a guest at the Sheraton to schmoose at Manuel's, fear not. There seems to be lots of parking in the area. Grapes is open from noon to 10 p.m., Monday through Friday, 10 to 10 on Saturdays, and from 12:30 to 6:30 p.m. on Sundays. 433-2333.

Fertitta's Delicatessen
1124 Howell St.
Shreveport, La.   424-5508

Next stop, Shreveport at lunchtime. Bountiful bevies of surprisingly beautiful girls wandering around downtown. What are they doing in Shreveport, which is, after all, approximately equidistant from Texarkana and Natchitoches?

Resisting a terrible urge to head north toward Gin City, Arkansas, I left the downtown area for 1124 Howell Street, home of Fertitta's Delicatessen, and northwesternmost outpost of the "Muffy" that I encountered.

Alas, lunchtime at Fertitta's is a mini-scaled version of the siege of Leningrad. It must have been the ungodly heat. In my wanderings in downtown Shreveport I did not realize that there were no other restaurants in the city. At least no other restaurants open for lunch. It also occurred to me later that lunchtime in Shreveport would be the ideal time to commit a major crime downtown, since the *entire* Shreveport police department was having lunch at Fertitta's along with at least three-quarters of the city's population of 182,064 (1970 Census). And Fertitta's is a pretty small place. Since I was anxious to press on to Dallas, I did not hang around. As it turned out, I should have hung around. Or gone to Gin City instead.

My EENT test showed it to be a smaller version of the places in the French Market, but with tables. Signs proclaimed the viands to be Italian, Greek and Syrian, with beer, wine and catering. 424-5508.

Hickory Ridge Farms
Rt. 1
Gladewater   984-9060

Welcome to Texas. If you enter the Lone Star State westbound on Interstate 20, don't think you're having a *deja vu* experience regarding the Poconos when you see the Hickory Ridge Farms Smoked Meats sign at the Joy/Wright Mt. exit. (Full home-20 is Rt. 1, Gladewater, Texas.)

Manager C. W. Wilson will assure you that you're in Texas, and after talking to him for a while, you'll know you can't be anywhere else.

Hickory Ridge is a Texas-size place with a vast assortment of smoked meats — among them hams, turkeys, beef and bacon. C. W. will give you the whole story. They're processed and smoked over green hickory wood by descendants of German settlers in the Dallas area.

Whatever you want — including a full array of sausages, other deli meats and cheeses — C. W. will ask you if you want him to "Set it out or put in on wheels?"

If you don't want it on wheels, there are a couple of tables in the main store, an intimate California Wine Room, and a large adjoining porch area.

Wine and beer are available, including Coors. (Hickory Ridge is about the farthest eastern point in Texas that you can buy the Colorado Kool-Aid.)

There's draft root beer and other soft drinks, including Dr Pepper, of course. For a long-lasting nosh, try the beef jerky. It's the real thing, like C. W. used to carry in his saddlebag.

Lots of imported and domestic groceries are on view at Hickory Ridge, too, including many with a Tex–Mex flavor. Among other things in the souvenir section, you'll find "I'm not a cowboy, I just found the hat" bumper stickers.

Hickory Ridge is open from 7 to 7 six days a week. (Closed Mondays.) 984-9060.

Sol's Deli and Turf Bar
1515 Commerce St.
Dallas   747-7977

As in too many other cities, it seems that downtown delis in Dallas have
almost disappeared. I did find one open, though — Sol's Deli and Turf
Bar at 1515 Commerce Street.

Sol's bar serves wine and beer, and the deli section has sandwiches
and pizza to stay or go.

Sol's is open from 10:30 'til 9 (5 on Saturdays) and is closed all day
Sundays. 747-7977.

Not visited, but recommended by Dallas sources are these: **Phil's
Oak Lawn Delicatessen, 3531 Oak Lawn; Wall's Delicatessen & Catering,
10749 Preston Road, and Khalil's Beirut Restaurant, 31 Highland Park
Shopping Village.**

The Delicatessen
112 E. 7th St.
Amarillo

They — or, rather — it, hasn't moved out of downtown Amarillo,
however. After driving through a couple of red dust storms in the
Panhandle, The Delicatessen at 112 East 7th Street is a cool and
welcome oasis.

Each day, a different specialty from a different country is offered,
plus regular fare. The international flavor comes through from this
smattering of items gleaned from the big wall menu: pastitsio, Polish
sausage, cordon bleu, kota, pita, submarines, egg rolls, wurst, Coney
Island hot dog, borscht, trout and garlic sauce, corned beef, and bagels
and lox. Eat in, or take out.

The Delicatessen is open from 8 to 5:30 ('til 3 on Saturdays), and
closed Sundays. No alcoholic beverages. And you don't have to say,
"I'm not here." There's no phone.

(End of Southern Odyssey)

ARIZONA

Out West
1481 South Milton
Flagstaff   774-0737

Flagstaff, Arizona, has lots of motels. I don't know how it got started, but I would guess because of its proximity to the Grand Canyon. Other natural wonders abound in the area, such as Humphrey Peak, the highest point in Arizona; Sunset Crater National Monument; the Arizona Snow Bowl Winter Sports Area; Lowell Observatory and Northern Arizona University. It's also the county seat of Coconino County and is on Interstate 40.

As the Arizona highway billboards proclaim, "As long as you're this close to the Grand Canyon, why don't you drop in?" And as long as you're in Flagstaff, you could drop into Out West at 1481 South Milton. It has standard deli sandwiches, combo submarines and salads. No alcoholic beverages. Open 10 a.m. to 10 p.m. seven days a week. 774-0737.

Hint: If you stay in Flagstaff and are heading for the south rim of the Canyon during the High Season, leave early in the morning to beat the Abominable Campers and take 89 and 64 north. You'll go through part of the Navajo Reservation where lots of little stands sell beadwork. To avoid backtracking, you can take 64 south (it goes in all directions) to Williams, or cut off on 180 if you insist upon going back to Flagstaff. Whatever turns you on, as long as you don't hurt anybody.

Hint II: Flagstaff's (the natives call it Flag) Park Plaza Motel's Speakeasy disco has unbelievably low prices during its happy hour(s), and its adjoining restaurant is unbelievably posh, considering the territory. Tell Denise the barmaid that I sent you.

Frank's New York Style Delicatessen
2301 W. Orange Dr.
Phoenix   242-8288

New York is represented again in Phoenix, this time Italian-style, at Frank's New York Style Delicatessen, 2301 West Orange Drive, a block north of Camelback Road.

The accent is Italian, but other deli varieties are yours for the asking. Some of the specialties are homemade Italian sausage and meatballs, corned beef, roast beef, pastrami, tuna salad, steak and pepper and eggplant parmagiana.

Beer and wine are served. Open Monday-Friday from 10 a.m. to 7 p.m.; also open Saturdays in the winter. 242-8288.

New York Bagels & Bialys
4801 N. Central Ave.
Phoenix   265-0678

In this case, New York Bagels & Bialys is in Phoenix, Arizona, not New York. Kosher-style NYB & B is at 4801 N. Central Ave.

New York is well-represented, though, by Schmulka Bernstein products that are imported. NYB & B also has been described as a sports-minded, old-fashioned, hang-out type of place that has an appeal to New Yorkers.

NYB & B does its own baking, including cheesecake and what a dutifully proud owner calls "the best bagels in the country."

Sit down or take it out. (Food only — no alcoholic beverages served.) Open 6:30 a.m. to 7:30 p.m. Mondays through Thursdays; 'til 8:30 on Fridays and Saturdays; closed Sundays at 2 p.m. Closed Thanksgiving, Yom Kippur, Christmas and New Year's. 265-0678.

CALIFORNIA

**Nate 'n Al Delicatessen & Restaurant
414 N. Beverly Dr.
Beverly Hills   274-0101**

Beverly Hills is a posh place, and so is the Nate 'n Al Delicatessen & Restaurant at 414 North Beverly Drive. It's a good place for celebrity-watching, if that's your bag, as well as a good place to eat.

Nate 'n Al's does a big breakfast business, with writers' conferences every morning. (I didn't see anybody watching them, except maybe the cashier.)

The place has been in business 31 years, and Al Mendelson and his son Barry are now the owners. Al says a lot of people, visitors and those living in the LA area, consider it a home away from home. Many of them drop in four or five days a week, and one visiting couple recently ate there two or three times a day while visiting Shakeytown.

Nate 'n Al's does a big take-out business, too, as evidenced by its contingent of 18 countermen. Al won't let anything frozen into his store. He prides himself on his products' freshness. For instance, every batch of potato salad is made to order.

His own recommendations include chopped liver, chicken in the pot, boiled beef, short ribs, brisket and potato pancakes.

Open seven days a week 7:30 - 9; 'til 10 on Saturdays. Closed High Holidays. Beer and wine served. 274-0101.

Canter's Fairfax Restaurant, Delicatessen and Bakery
419 N. Fairfax Ave.
Los Angeles   651-2030

The full name is Canter's Fairfax Restaurant, Delicatessen and Bakery, a West Hollywood institution at 419 North Fairfax Avenue, which is itself some kind of institution.

When there was a Lyndy's in the east, Canter's was called "the Lyndy's of the west." It's owned by 84-year-old Ben Canter and his family. It is reported that the family patriarch arrives each morning at 3 or 4 o'clock for an on-site inspection.

Canter's is a big place, with an adjoining bar and lounge, the Kibitz Room. It cures its own beef, and makes its own pickles when the right kind of cucumber is available. It has its own bakery, and does a brisk business at the bakery counter. Many regulars go for the steaming kaiser rolls in the morning.

As might be expected, Canter's has a huge sandwich selection. Its menu notes, "One sandwich not enough? Two too many? Try one and one-half, and you won't leave any." Also as might be expected, the "Special Sandwiches" are named after people, places and things. For instance, Eddie Cantor's Delight, Mickey Katz Gourmet, Fisherman's Folly, Bronx Special, a Little New Yorker and a Big New Yorker, plus a Danny Thomas and a Danny Thomas #2.

A la carte and complete dinners are served. Choose from a variety of appetizers, including knishes. You can have any of several varieties of chicken soup, barley bean, or beet or cabbage borscht. Then consider a couple of dozen entrees. A few are stuffed bell pepper, kishka, fried kreplach, turkey giblets, gefilte fish, blintzes, cold boiled fish, roast tongue, baby beef liver, and steaks — broiled salmon or New York cut. Wash it down with something from the fountain. Maybe a chocolate or cherry phosphate? Beer, wine and cocktails also are available.

Canter's does catering, and will bake a cake for your birthday, wedding or Bar Mitzvah. It's open 24 hours, closed on the High Holidays. 651-2030. Canter's prices are reasonable, and there's free parking.

As long as you're parking free, take a look at Fairfax Avenue. A venerable patron of the Kibitz Room called it "Matzo Ball Lane." You can get your share of matzo balls there, but there's lots more: A Hungarian and a Yugoslav restaurant; the Venice; Orthodox butchers; "New York Italian cuisine," and the Tel Aviv, King David and Eilat restaurants. You can also find gifts from Israel, places that serve falafel, bakeries and the offices of the Jewish Daily Forward.

Carmel Kosher Deli
443 N. Fairfax
Los Angeles   658-5046

At 443 North Fairfax is the Carmel Kosher Deli. Specialty of the house is "Aloof Carmel," Israeli-style fried chicken in a basket.

The Carmel is open from 9 to 9, but closed Saturdays and all Jewish holidays. Take-outs and catering, too. 658-5046.

Langer's Delicatessen and Restaurant
704 S. Alvarado St.
Los Angeles   483-8050

At 704 South Alvarado Street near downtown Los Angeles is Langer's Delicatessen and Restaurant, a place that has grown six-fold in seating capacity alone since it started operating in 1947.

Langer's menu is Olympian-length, with the lead item pastrami. You can have it in a multitude of forms and combinations, even barbecued. Another unusual barbecue specialty is cod served with cream cheese as a cold plate or sandwich. The cod-cream cheese combination is also available with whitefish and lox. It comes with onions, tomatoes, ripe olives and bagels.

There are at least 18 more deli plates with meat or fish; hot, cold or French dip sandwiches; salads and a category called "Something Special." Among the latter offerings are tomato herring, kishka, knishes (with or without gravy), kasha varnishkes, a chicken liver omelette and spaghetti and meatballs. Langer's breakfast menu also is extensive, and diverse – among its listings are kippers, matzo brei, ham and eggs and hot cakes.

Soups include chicken combinations, and on weekends, barley mushroom with giblets. A daily special entree is beef stew. Some others are corned beef and cabbage, lamb shank, liver and onions, veal (Parmesan and cutlet), braised ox joints, sauteed chicken livers, gefilte fish, shrimp, halibut and a variety of steaks.

Langer's does its own baking, with whipped cream cake a specialty. You can also get noodle kugel for dessert. Imported and domestic beers are served, as is buttermilk. Take-outs are available, and Langer's does a big catering business.

Langer's is open from 6:30 to 1, Sundays through Thursdays, and until 3 on Fridays and Saturdays. It's closed on Yom Kippur and Thanksgiving. It has a 60-car parking lot. 483-8050.

David's
474 Geary St.
San Francisco   771-1600

San Francisco is a compact city, ideal for walking if you can handle the hills. Downtown, however, on an almost-level block of Geary Street, you can be kind to your legs and your stomach because three of the city's top delis are located within a matzo ball's throw of each other. They're between Mason and Taylor Streets, a block from Union Square, and opposite the two major legitimate theaters, the Geary and the Curran.

David's, at 474 Geary, was the first deli in downtown San Francisco, beginning with three stools in 1954. Owner David Apfelbaum did all his own cooking for the first year. And some of the cooks he hired then are still with him. Waitresses have built up seniority, too — some as long as 18 years. The pastry chef — a 21-year veteran — was formerly at the Hotel Sacher in Vienna, and his creations at David's would be a credit to the venerable Austrian hospice.

Try the cheese cake, mocha bee hives, rum balls, strudels, macaroons and more, more, especially the pastry *piece de resistance* – the Napoleon. Get fat already, break out in zitzes, but it's delicious.

All right, don't start with dessert. Do what I did one memorable evening. Start with kishka (also memorable). Some alternative appetizers are lox with onions, gefilte fish, chopped chicken livers (with schmaltz), three different kinds of herring, maybe even fruit cocktail?

Next, cold beet borscht with sour cream. Lots of other soups available, including cabbage borscht, cold schav, split pea, Hungarian potato and chicken, of course, with matzo balls, noodles or kreplach.

Now are you ready to eat? I had the baked brisket, but you don't have to be a copycat. Ask the waitress what the special of the day is, or read the menu. You can have boiled chicken (leg or breast) with horseradish, stuffed jellied carp, Hungarian goulash, sauerbraten, stuffed cabbage, cheese or meat blintzes. You can even get kosher Chicago frankfurters (with bread and pickle, or with beans or salad.) On Wednesdays only, there's corned beef and cabbage. (Next time St. Patrick's Day falls on a Wednesday, you know where to go.)

Some of the desserts I've already mentioned. Wash it all down with a variety of drinks, including Dr. Brown's Cel-Ray tonic. Draft and imported bottled beer are available. There's a special rate on dry Israeli wine with the complete dinner. As David says, it's imported, how else? You also get a basket of bread and bagels.

Enough dinner? Save room for breakfast. If you want to go all the way, have the lox, onion and three eggs. Quantitatively lesser amounts of morning fare also are listed. But I have one quibble with David's menu. A bagel with *marmalade?* Would you put mayonnaise on pastrami? *Chacun a son gout,* je suppose.

For lunch, you could do what I did one day – get a lox and cream cheese on poppy seed bagel, put it on wheels, go to the end of Geary Boulevard and nosh while watching the seals cavort on the rocks. You can't do that in Skokie, or even on Seventh Avenue.

If you'd rather eat in, choose from an array of hot and cold dishes (including dairy), or sandwiches ranging from a frankfurter to sturgeon. You might want to try something on Siberian soldier's bread or chale.

Where to sit? As you enter the main entrance of David's, a sign tells you: "There are two rooms you can't see: The Celebrity Corner & The Big Room ... with tables, chairs, waitresses, etc." (The large counter you can see.)

The walls of the Celebrity Corner are lined, appropriately, with photos of celebrities. David is having all of them reduced to accommodate more. One of his favorites is Sammy Davis, who has large amounts of David's kishka exported to Lake Tahoe when he's appearing there. Another is Topol. David says the popular Israeli actor doesn't eat anywhere else in San Francisco.

According to David, some would-be celebrities dine on a hot dog elsewhere and then parade outside his place while munching on tooth-picks in an attempt to impress the girls passing by.

Upstairs, a room formerly used only for catering is being remodeled into another dining room called "Above David's." Above "Above David's" is the Hotel David. (He was impressed by the song "If I Had My Life to Live Over, I'd Live Over a Delicatessen," so he bought the hotel.) Guests receive a complimentary "Executive Breakfast" from the deli, and a 10 percent discount on other meals.

David's is open from 8 — 1 Sunday through Thursday, and 8 — 3 Friday and Saturday. Closed Rosh Hashanah and Yom Kippur. 771-1600.

Fox's
706 Mission St.
San Francisco   392-9096

A few blocks from the "theater district," at 706 Mission Street, is Fox's, which I couldn't check out because it was closed for vacation while I was in San Francisco.

Sources say that it draws an almost exclusively local trade, which doesn't sound bad. It's also next door to a reasonably priced parking lot with a friendly proprietor. 392-9096.

The House of Bagels
5030 Geary Blvd.
San Francisco   752-6000

Recommended even for emigre New Yorkers are the bagels from The House of Bagels, 5030 Geary Boulevard. Ask for Moishe the Bay Gull. The House of Bagels also produces a miniature variety which might be enjoyed by babies who are teething. 752-6000.

Solomon's Restaurant & Deli
410 Geary St.
San Francisco   776-3525

Mr. and Mrs. Solomon were away when I visited their establishment —
Solomon's Restaurant & Deli — at 410 Geary Street — so I did not have
the benefit of hearing their personal experiences in the deli business.

My Bay Area informants tell me they're a delightful couple who have
been in business about as long as David Apfelbaum.

Their place is smaller than David's or the Stage, and "modestly
priced" as their business card states. It also says, "Just Like Mama Used
to Cook."

In addition to the usual deli items, Solomon's features five-course
dinners and daily specials. Sit at the counter or in the dining area.
Take-outs, too.

Solomon's is open from 8 - 3 a.m. weekdays, 'til 1 a.m. Sundays, 365
days a year. 776-3525.

Stage Delicatessen
424 Geary St.
San Francisco   776-8968

The year-old Stage Delicatessen, at 424 Geary, is a busy place, with a
large adjoining bar and cocktail lounge that offers piano bar-type entertainment in the evening. If you like piano bars, this block of Geary
Street is loaded with them. If you want to pub crawl, it might be a
better idea to deli crawl, too, noshing before, during, and after at the
Stage, David's and Solomon's. But back to the deli side of the Stage.

Just like home, there are salamis hanging and drying for those
customers who like them extra ripe. Owner Fred Del Marva is justly
proud of his bialys, and says the Stage is the only place on the West
Coast that serves the rolls.

Among the Stage's star attractions are its triple decker sandwiches.
(Ingredients total three-quarters of a pound.) You can choose from six
combinations, but I give the leading role to "Fred's Special": Hot
corned beef, chopped chicken liver, roast turkey and imported Swiss
with cole slaw and Russian dressing. All the triple deckers come with a
side order of cole slaw or potato salad, a kosher dill, and are served on
rye, Russian pumpernickel, or challe.

If you're not up to a triple decker, try one of the "Dynamic Duos":
Choose a combination of any two items from nine meats and smoked
salmon. They're served on twin French rolls with potato salad, cole
slaw, baked beans, or french fries. (If you're in a party of five, you can
taste a little bit of everything.)

And that's not all. The Stage offers a huge sandwich list, including lake sturgeon when available. The hot open face varieties come with potato kugel if desired. (You should desire.) The bagel, Nova, whitefish, sturgeon and cream cheese combinations also are served open-faced, and well-garnished. You also can get cold platters.

A la carte and complete dinners range from frankfurters or potato pancakes to a Romanian tenderloin or New York cut shell steak. Among the variety in between are kasha varnishkes, gefilte fish, stuffed cabbage or bell peppers, short ribs, Hungarian goulash, chicken (including chicken in the pot), baked brisket, meatloaf, London broil and homemade meat or cheese blintzes (1½ pounds.) Potato kugel with almost everything.

Appetizers include homemade kishka, chopped chicken livers, gefilte fish, stuffed cabbage, herring and fruit cocktail. Outstanding among the soups is hot Ukrainian cabbage borscht (sweet and sour). Desserts feature pastries baked on the premises. Beer, wine and cocktails are available. If you get there early, try the matzo brey breakfast special, or the brunch that includes a Ramos Fizz.

The Stage also has take-outs and does catering. It's open from 7 – 1, 365 days a year. 776-8968.

The Bagel
1300 Polk St.
San Francisco   441-2212

At 1300 Polk Street (corner of Bush) is The Bagel. It's in a shopping, dining, drinking and looking area known as Polk Gulch, or to some, "The Greenwich Village of the West." The California Street cable car stops a couple of blocks away.

The Bagel is cafeteria-style, with a good seating capacity. Owner Leo England says The Bagel is noted for its soups, and offers an "International Soup Experience" featuring Austrian, Russian, Jewish, and Polish varieties.

It also might be the westernmost point in the contiguous states where one can get piroshki. Also on hand are knishes, kosher Polish sausage, Hungarian goulash, Swiss bockwurst, baked brisket, kishka, blintzes and Dr. Brown's Cel-Ray tonic.

All kinds of sandwiches, of course. Siberian soldier's bread, too. There are chickens barbecuing in the window, and an ice cream section, including cones if you want to drip on Polk Street.

There is a long list of desserts. Beer, wine, take-outs available. The Bagel is open from 8 to 1, 365 days a year. 441-2212.

The Deli
1980 Union St.
San Franscico   563-7274

The Deli, 1980 Union Street, is in a trendy section of shops, galleries and restaurants. The front page of its menu says that The Deli is "Where you can brunch, lunch, dine, sup, and nosh in splendor, or carry it all away."

"Splendor" is not used hyperbolically. It is a splendid-looking place, maybe even posh or opulent. But fear not, the prices do not match the architecture or decor. They're in line for San Francisco.

The Deli is in a San Francisco Victorian-style house. The interior is elaborately decorated, with stained glass skylights, a garden section with sliding glass roofs, plants, flowers and artwork. Entering it on a bright day produces a kaleidoscopic effect.

But this is not 1,001 Decorating Ideas, so let's look at the food. There is a good selection of sandwiches, including many standard deli items, Lola's chicken salad and a brisket French dip.

There are soups and cold platters, a couple of "calorie counters," a deli chef's salad, and appetizers and side dishes that include chopped liver, gefilte fish and kishka.

Entrees include roast brisket, stuffed cabbage rolls, knockwurst and sauerkraut, bratwurst and red cabbage, meat and cheese blintzes, baked short ribs, sweet and sour meat balls, baked chicken and roast beef. Some are served with mushroom rice. There is also a daily dinner feature.

For dessert, try berries and cream, French pastries, a deli sundae, or a green lagoon. Milkshakes and malteds also are available, and there is complete bar service.

The Deli is open Sunday through Thursday from 11 to 12:45, 'til 1:15 on Friday and Saturday. Bar stays open until 2. 563-7274.

If you're looking for strictly kosher food in the Bay Area, David Apfelbaum tells me that it's available at the Hillel House at the University of California Campus at Berkeley.

Haiman's Delicatessen and Restaurant
412 University
San Diego   295-5222

Haiman's Delicatessen and Restaurant, 412 University, San Diego, is the "Home of the Original Sportsman Sandwich." Named after local teams, the jumbo sandwiches feature fresh-cut deli delicacies, including Nova. Has anybody ever said, "Charge me a Charger?"

Both sit-down and take-out, Haiman's also does extensive catering. The 20-year-old establishment is located near San Diego's Hotel Circle, Convention Center and hospital complexes. Imported and domestic beer and wine are served.

It's open from 8 to 6, six days. (Closed Sundays.) 295-5222.

COLORADO

Richman's Delicatessen Restaurant
323 14th St.
Denver   892-0212

Richman's Delicatessen Restaurant is in downtown Denver at 323 14th Street. It's mostly sandwich-oriented.

The oldies but goodies are available, including bagels and lox. But in keeping with its western location, you can also get barbecued beef or burritos.

Richman's does its own baking; has carry-outs and a good seating capacity, and serves 3.2 beer. It's open 7:30 to 4 p.m.; closed Saturdays, Sundays and national holidays. 892-0212.

The Bagel Delicatessen and Restaurant
6439 E. Hampten   756-6667
6217 E. 14th Ave.   322-0350
Denver

The Bagel Delicatessen and Restaurant has two locations in Denver — 6439 East Hampten and 6217 East 14th Avenue.

Both feature sandwiches, with corned beef and pastrami the lead items. Homemade soups are served, too.

They're open for eat-in and carry-out from 8 a.m. to 8 p.m. seven days a week. Closed Jewish holidays. 756-6667 (East Hampten); 322-0350 (East 14th Avenue).

CONNECTICUT

The Atlantic Market
350 Hope
Stamford   327-8283

The Atlantic Market, 350 Hope, Stamford, Connecticut, is so clean and so German, it's almost intimidating. ("We have ways of dealing with people who don't eat our Black Forest ham.")

Some of the world's best-looking meat stares out from the counter, and the store (take-out only) carries a large variety of sausages and imported German delicacies.

Sandwiches-to-go are a big item. (I dutifully consumed my Black Forest ham on German rye while tooling down the Merritt Parkway. It was very good, Fritz, honest!)

The Atlantic Market is open five days from 8 — 6 (Fridays 'til 7) and closed Sundays. 327-8283.

Rein's N.Y. Style Deli-Restaurant
428 Hartford Turnpike and Hartford Civic Center
Hartford (2 locations)
East Brook Mall   875-0944 — 527-1894
Mansfield   423-6460

Rein's N.Y. Style Deli-Restaurant has three locations in central Connecticut — 428 Hartford Turnpike (Exit 96 off I-86), the Hartford Civic Center and East Brook Mall, Route 195, Mansfield.

Rein's imports Hebrew National products from New York and features corned beef, pastrami, tongue and kosher turkey.

The extensive menu lists a wide variety of hot and cold dishes, from full meals to snacks, with plenty of desserts.

Many of Mama and Papa Rein's family recipes are utilized, including kugel, salads, stuffed cabbage and rum cake.

Take-out and catering services available, including cocktail knishes.

The I-86 location is open Monday-Thursday from 9 to 9; Friday, from 9 to 1 a.m.; Saturday, 9 to 2 a.m.; Sunday, 8 to 9. 875-0944.

Civic Center branch open 24 hours, 527-1894; Mansfield, 9:30 - 10, Friday and Saturday 'til 11. 423-6460.

(May be closed half days on some holidays. Check on Passover, Rosh Hashanah, Yom Kippur.)

WASHINGTON, D.C. and environs

Baltimore Delicatessen
1101 Bladensburg Rd. N.E.
Washington, D.C.   399-1111

According to Manny Leichtman, who owns the Baltimore Delicatessen in Washington, his place does not attract too many politicians, even though it's only 15 or 20 minutes away from the Capitol (1101 Bladensburg Road N.E.). That might be recommendation enough to visit the Baltimore, especially if you've just left the Congressional galleries.

Manny says that he does get a good media trade, however. Who's that behind the pastrami? It's Deep Throat!

The Baltimore, a 40-year-old deli, specializes in kosher-style food and cooks its own corned beef. It also does its own baking. Some of its specialties are homemade matzo ball and other soups, puddings, chopped chicken livers, combination sandwiches and Hungarian strudel. (Sit-down or to-go.) Imported and domestic beers are available.

Open 7 to 7, closed Sundays and holidays. 399-1111.

Katz's Super Market
4860 Bolling Brook Parkway
Rockville, Md.   468-0400

Somewhat farther away from the Capitol is Katz's Super Market at 4860 Bolling Brook Parkway, Rockville, Maryland. All its deli items are kosher, and you can sit down or take it away. Beer and wine to go only.

Katz's does its own baking, including rye breads and sweet items. It also features hot meals, sandwiches, knishes, kishka, and in the wintertime, soups.

Open 9 to 9 Sunday through Thursday. Closes early Friday and all day Saturday. 468-0400.

FLORIDA

Wolfie's Restaurant
1390 N.E. 163rd Street
Miami Beach   945-7525

Wolfie's is a grand old name in Miami Beach, and there are at least three establishments there at the present time that bear that designation. All are independently owned.

Heading from the north to escape the cold, the first you'll run into is Wolfie's Restaurant at 1390 N.E. 163rd Street, a couple of miles off Motel Row in a residential district. It combines a restaurant, bakery, deli and gourmet shop, and is noted for its homemade pastries, including croissants.

If you want something more substantial than a continental breakfast, have a sandwich or stop by for a full-course lunch or dinner. Among the favorites are beef and chicken in the pot and stuffed cabbage.

According to owner Bernie Schandler, large portions are the rule, and very large shrimp are featured. Buckets of garnishes are provided, and there is full bar service.

Hours are 7 a.m. until 2 a.m., except for Sundays, when closing time is 1 a.m. Closed Yom Kippur. 945-7525.

Wolfie's Sandwich Shop
21st & Collins
Miami Beach   538-6626

Wolfie's at 21st and Collins, Miami Beach (Celebrity Corner), is well known for its omelettes served after 10 p.m.

It also has traditional sandwiches, stuffed cabbage, beef stew, brisket, chicken in the pot and goulash. Cheesecake and pastries are home-baked, as are the bagels. Beer is served. Open 24 hours. 538-6626.

Wolfie's Sandwich Shop
195 Lincoln Road
Miami Beach   538-0326

Farthest south is Wolfie's at 195 Lincoln Road, Miami Beach. It does its own cooking and baking, and features cheesecake, corned beef and allied deli delights. No booze.

Open seven days a week from 6:45 a.m. until 12:45 a.m. 538-0326.

H & M Stein's Delicatessen
1139 Washington Avenue
Miami Beach   534-2557

Stein's is located at 1139 Washington Avenue, across from Miami Beach's City Hall, so it's handy if you're paying a parking ticket.

Strictly kosher, Stein's does its own cooking and baking, and is proud of its gefilte fish. Eat in, or take out. No liquor.

Hours are 11 a.m. - 8:30 p.m. but Stein's is closed Friday night and Saturday. 534-2557.

Cracker Barrel
1361 3rd St. S.
Naples   262-6311

If you'd like to try a Coral Snake's Temptation or a Skunk Ape's Delight, the place to go is the Cracker Barrel at 1361 Third Street South in Naples, Florida.

The exotically named delicacies mentioned above are two of the Cracker Barrel's "Great Overstuffed Sandwiches." They are, respectively, corned beef and Genoa salami with tomato, lettuce and onion, covered with Russian dressing; and baked ham, Genoa salami and Swiss cheese, topped with lettuce, onion, garlic oil and hot peppers. (The "real" Skunk Ape is Florida's equivalent of the Yeti or Bigfoot.)

If you don't want any of the pre-named specials, the Cracker Barrel says, "You design it and we'll build it." Choose from a dozen meats and cheeses, several breads and rolls, and a variety of garnishes. Salads and chili are available, as is beer.

The Cracker Barrel is located three blocks from the beach, and its decor, featuring rough-cut cypress, is in keeping with its southwest Florida location. It's open from 10 to 6 Mondays through Saturdays. Closed Sundays. 262-6311.

GEORGIA

Cloudt's Food Store & Village Kitchen
1937 Peachtree Road N.E.
Atlanta   355-7523

Cloudt's is reportedly Atlanta's original catering establishment. It's at 1937 Peachtree Road N.E., with a meat department down the block at No. 1919.

The big seller in its terrace restaurant is fried chicken, especially at lunch. It's also noted for salads, and does a large take-out business, including imports. No beer or wine.

Cloudt's has a "European Country" look and is open from 9 a.m. until 6:30 p.m. Monday through Saturday. Closed Sundays and holidays. 355-7523.

Fiddler on the Mezzanine
231 Peachtree St. N.E.
Atlanta   658-1222

Would you believe a fancy-schmancy deli that also serves *grits?* Believe.
It's Fiddler on the Mezzanine in Atlanta's Peachtree Center (231 Peachtree Street N.E.).

Decorwise, Fiddler cheerfully features butcher block tables and ac-
cents. It's open for breakfast, lunch and dinner, with specials at all
meals. Carry-outs, party trays and catering are available, plus delivery
within five blocks of Peachtree Center. Also private dining and meeting
rooms.

Besides grits, in this oasis in the Heart of the New South you'll find a
copious variety of the good old standbys. (Which may even be eaten by
Good Old Boys.) Fiddler purveys overstuffed, combination and hot open
faced sandwiches; assorted fish and meat platters; dairy dishes; soups
and salads.

Among the evening offerings are chicken or beef flanken in the pot;
steaks (including Romanian tenderloin); liver; pan fried trout and surf
and turf. Daily specials, too.

In addition to regular fare, Sunday brunch includes such items as
noodle kugel, kasha varnishkes and barbecued salmon. If you have a
very young deli maven in your midst, bring him/her. Brunch is free for
kids under eight.

There is an ice cream fountain and beer and wine are served. During
late afternoon and early evening weekdays, a "happy hour" features
cheese and fruit with wine.

Fiddler is open Monday through Thursday from 7:30 - 10; Friday
7:30 - 11:30; Saturday 8 - 11:30; Sunday 8 - 9 (Sunday brunch served
10:30 - 3.) 658-1222.

Happy Herman's
2299 Cheshire Bridge Road N.E.
Atlanta   321-3012

Greenbriar Shopping Center
Atlanta   344-5782

Happy Herman's, which stocks 75 meats and 150 cheeses, has two
locations in Atlanta. They're at 2299 Cheshire Bridge Road N.E. and the
Greenbriar Shopping Center.

The Cheshire store is take-out only, but you can go either way in the
shopping center spot, which also has a cafeteria-style restaurant.

Happy Herman's has been around for 30 years, and specializes in meats, cheeses, sausage, wines and international gourmet foods. Beer is served at the Greenbriar restaurant.

Hours are 9 a.m. to 11 p.m. The Greenbriar location is closed on Sundays, when the Cheshire location closes at 9 p.m. Both are closed on Christmas. 321-3012 (Cheshire); 344-5782 (Greenbriar).

Henri's Bakery
61 Irby Avenue N.E.
Atlanta   237-0202

Henri's Bakery — at 61 Irby Avenue N.E. in Atlanta — is designed for take-out only, but if you want, you can stand up and eat your sandwich while admiring one of the old showcases.

Mrs. Bell says that her Po' Boys sell by the thousands. There are other sandwiches made from home-cooked meat or imports from Milwaukee. The onion bun is especially recommended. All breads and pastries are home-baked. No beer or wine.

Catering services are available. Henri's is open from 9 a.m. until 6:30 p.m. on weekdays, from 10 a.m. until 5 p.m. on Sundays, and is closed on major national holidays. 237-0202.

Harry Baron Delicatessen-Restaurant
3500 Peachtree Road N.E.
Atlanta   261-5288

Kosher-style Harry Baron's is another Atlanta establishment on Peachtree Road N.E. — at No. 3500.

In addition to sandwiches, you can get other traditional deli fare such as stuffed cabbage, blintzes, pancakes, and homemade soups. Beer is served.

Platters and catering available. Weekday hours are 7:45 a.m. until midnight ('til 1 a.m. Saturdays), and Sundays from 9:30 a.m. until 7:30 p.m. Closed major national holidays. 261-5288.

HAWAII

The Deli
Butler's Pantry
Patti's Chinese Kitchen
Lyn's Delicatessen
Kabuki Restaurant and Delicatessen
Kenny's Delicatessen
Ricco's Old World Delicatessen
(see below for address)

Interstate 80 does not extend west to Hawaii, so the following listings were supplied by a knowledgeable Islands source:

The Deli, 2232 Kalakaua, Honolulu (Waikiki) is an internationally known delicatessen that draws people from the mainland as well as local customers. Although it specializes in kosher-style foods, its owners are Bobby and Mimi Mau, who are Chinese.

Butler's Pantry is a gourmet deli located at Shop 1066, Ala Moana Center, Honolulu.

Also in Ala Moana Center are Patti's Chinese Kitchen (Cantonese cuisine,) and Lyn's Delicatessen (kosher-style).

Kabuki Restaurant and Delicatessen, 98-020 Kam Highway, Aiea, serves authentic Japanese foods.

Kenny's Delicatessen specializes in local-style hot plate lunches. 1620 North School Street, Honolulu.

Recommended on the island of Maui is Ricco's Old World Delicatessen in the Whalers Village in Lahaina.

Aloha.

ILLINOIS

Ada's Fishery & Corned Beef Center
4407 N. Kedzie Ave.
Chicago   539-5363-64

Make no mistake: fame is the name of the game at Ada's (4407 N. Kedzie). Virtually every dish is prefaced by the word "famous," even the sailors and bathers special. *The* special, however, is the Lazy Susan for home use. It features assorted cold cuts and dairy products. But the big buys here are made in corned beef (part of Ada's legal name), and lox. Ada's president, Mr. Morris Weiner (named the joint after his first wife), maintains a New York style of operation; no serving on the premises. Ada's is open from 7 a.m. to 7 p.m. seven days a week. 539-5363-64.

Ashkeys
1432 W. Morse
Chicago   465-5392

A restaurant cum deli at 1432 W. Morse, formerly Ashkenaz, the popular take-out deli items here are corned beef, turkey, roast beef, tongue and salami. They also are available on the restaurant side. Typical deli fare such as matzo ball soup, kreplach, and blintzes also is available. You ever heard of a Joey Bishop? It's a three story corned beef and Swiss cheese sandwich. Hours are 6 a.m. to 11 p.m. Sunday through Thursday; 6 a.m. to midnight Friday and Saturday. No booze. 465-5392.

Braverman's
1604 W. Chicago Ave.
Chicago   421-3979

For more than three decades Chicago's hungry have depended upon Braverman's, 1604 W. Chicago Ave., for deli delights such as chicken soup and corned beef and pastrami, the latter being the establishment's best sellers, as they are at most delis. But Braverman's is known for the huge quantities of meat piled between bread — seven ounces the serving. Braverman's, owned for the last eight years by Zeno Pappas, a Greek Cypriot, bones and cures its own meats. Zeno eschews all frozen foods and the local critics rate his offerings with several stars in most of the Chicago guidebooks. Among favorites in the cafeteria cum dining room deli are potato pancakes and bowls of the ever simmering chicken soup (there are three fresh soups daily.) Braverman's, a favorite of local media personalities, claims to export tons of corned beef and pastrami to such faraway places as Acapulco and New York City. Zeno says he provided the fixins for a St. Patrick's Day party in British Columbia last year but is proudest of the fact that for several years Braverman's has served up 2,000 sandwiches annually for plumber's union meetings. Braverman's is open from 10 a.m. to 8 p.m. Monday through Friday. 421-3979.

Caesar's Food Store
901 N. Damen Ave.
Chicago   486-6190

For half a century Caesar's Polish deli has been located in this neighborhood (901 N. Damen Ave.) and if the current owner, Kathleen Optenheim, daughter of the founders, has her way, it will be here in the year
2001. This area used to be the hub of a near northeast side Polish
enclave, but the signs of decay pop through, unmasked even by the
stately Lombardy poplars that dot the neighborhood. Although the Poles
are moving away, Ms. Optenheim is making a determined effort to stem
the migration. Surely the taste of her *nalesniki* (a Polish crepe suzette
stuffed with apples, cheeses, plums, prunes or apricots) would be an
excellent reason to reconsider. And the specialty of the house, *pierogi,* a
dumpling with sauerkraut, meat, cheese, plum and potatoes, is yet
another. Other popular dishes are *paluszki,* or potato fingers, and *bigos,*
yclept hunter's stew (sauerkraut, cabbage and polish sausage), and the
savory soups, sauerkraut, beet, chicken and pea, available daily. Caesar's
is open from 9 a.m. to 6 p.m. weekdays and from 9 a.m. to 4 p.m.
Saturday; closed Sundays. 486-6190.

Grand Deli
164 E. Grand Ave.
Chicago   467-6310

What makes this deli grand? Partly it's the name of the street on which
it's located (164 E. Grand Ave.), partly it's the atmosphere of tempting
kosher foods and partly it's the good humor of the Roth family. The
former home of Jazz Ltd., a Second City musical landmark, the Grand
marks the return to the business — the deli trade, that is — by a
family that once dispensed similar fare a good many years ago on the
South Side. Everyone in the family works — patriarch Maury, wife
Anne, and sons Howard, Herb and Bob.

While the best sellers, predictably, are corned beef, roast beef and
pastrami, it was Mamma Roth's soup that made the place famous. The
late Hal Tate, memories of whom dot the walls in photographs, fell in
love with her sweet and sour cabbage soup. Tate, whose mark in the
world included a stint as host of one of radio's first talk shows, and a

similar triumph at the dawn of television, also was a newspaperman. He brought his media friends in to share his newfound gustatory delight and soon there were stories in the newspaper lauding the Grand's provisions. Several by-lined newspaper columnists can be found there in the late afternoons and on Saturday columnist and TV talk-show host Irv Kupcinet can be found noshing with *Sun-Times* colleagues.

At noontide, however, the lines flowing out of the deli, equalling about an eight or nine minute wait, are dappled by the ink-stained clothing of pressmen from nearby newspaper plants.

Among our personal favorites here are the soups, especially pea soup, which is made from scratch. Beer, at a reduced price with a meal, is available. The Grand Deli is open from 8 a.m. to 7 p.m. Monday through Friday and from 8 a.m. to 5 p.m. on Saturday; closed Sunday. 467-6310.

Jerry's Food & Liquors
215 E. Grand
Chicago   337-2500

If you're a masochist, you may want to try this place (at 215 E. Grand). But if you're not, you can do quite well elsewhere in this nabe. That doesn't mean the food isn't good. On the contrary, some of it, such as the corned beef sandwich, is above average. But Jerry's is a raucous eatery, the owner himself being by far the schrei-ingest. That provides what many Chicagoans call "atmosphere." If you don't immediately shout out your order as you enter, the owner shouts at you. And, as a matter of fact, if you're not stepping briskly as you approach the counter, you may very well be prodded just a bit.

The luncheon crowd here is much the same as that at the Grand Deli, virtually across the street — workingmen, principally pressmen from the Chicago Tribune. But the Grand's atmosphere is decidedly friendlier. Dining space at Jerry's is confined to stand-up counters. Carry-outs are available.

And, to be fair to the owner: the pastrami and boiled ham are pretty good, too. Schlep in any time other than lunch and the pace is less tense. Jerry holds forth daily from 6:30 a.m. to 6:30 p.m. and on Saturday from 6:30 a.m. to 1 p.m. Closed Sunday. 337-2500.

The Mallers Coffee Shop
5 S. Wabash Ave.
Chicago   263-7696

In the heart of Chicago's famed Loop barely two floors above the tracks of the roaring El is one dilly of a deli with an unlikely name: The Mallers Coffee Shop, 5 S. Wabash Ave. The Mallers building, from which the deli's name is derived, is known for its jewelry shops; their proprietors congregate in the booths early in the ayem weekdays and Saturday to discuss their business. It is not uncommon to hear such weighty topics as the day's quotes for gold, sold in troy ounces, amidst requests for more coffee.

One caveat: Without some guidance this deli may be hard to find. Using the Wabash entrance simply take the stairs to the third floor and you can't miss it. If you feel daring, try the antique elevators (they're worth a look even if you don't use them.)

Owner Sam Sennett says corned beef, chopped liver and dairy dishes are best sellers among his kosher-style offerings. Also popular are lox, gefilte fish — an everyday item — and, among other favorites, cheese blintzes. (Several soups also are delicious: kreplach, matzo dumpling and others with a chicken base.)

Lunch time here is frenetic. The several servers behind the counter seem constantly to be shouting at the waitresses, cooks in the kitchen, or, whoop! the patrons. However, there is no belligerence here, just a willingness to get a job done efficiently. Which, for the most part, gets done that way.

There's a large carry-out trade, but for the gentry the Mallers deli counter is ringed by stools and several booths. The waitresses are friendly and their service is swift. Food portions, in general, are satisfying. No booze. Hours are 7 a.m. to 5 p.m. daily; 7 a.m. to 2 p.m. Saturdays. 263-7696.

Manny's
1139 S. Jefferson
Chicago   939-2855

Traditional fare — kishka, knish, kreplach and kasha, etc. — aren't the only reason for the large clientele at Manny's (1139 S. Jefferson). It's the wide assortment of dishes served in whopping big portions. They include chicken pot pie (kreplach and kasha also come in chicken soup, incidentally), gefilte fish, roast veal breast, corned beef and cabbage, prune tzimmes and, would you believe? spaghetti and meat balls.

But back to traditional fare: corned beef piled on rye bread or on onion roll, ham, tongue, pastrami and roast beef also are popular.

Manny's cafeteria-style comestibles are favored by a whole host of diners from the area, ranging from firefighters from a local school to what you call your regular students and noontide shoppers struck with hunger.

Don't forget the desserts. The broad selection includes canned figs, baked apples, Napoleons and cream pies. No booze. Open 5 a.m. to 5:30 p.m. Monday through Saturday; closed Sunday. 939-2855.

Purple Pickle
3463½ N. Broadway
Chicago   549-7577

The Purple Pickle, 3463½ N. Broadway, looks pie-eyed. The walls are absolutely plastered . . . well, at least they're *painted* purple (whence the name?). But decor aside, there's fine fare among the six dozen or so sandwich offerings. Among top ranks are the brisket sandwich, complemented by several tempting soups (try the mushroom barley, thick and steamy), the ubiquitous corned beef, chopped liver and other standards. For some reason white bread is treated almost as if it were good, wholesome rye; ergo, specify the bread of your choice when ordering. 549-7577.

Selma's Delicatessen
2549 W. Devon
Chicago   AM 2-7391

There used to be several delightful delis on Devon. Selma's is one of the remaining handful. (Also remaining and reportedly worth visiting are Milt's, 2124 W. Devon, and the New York Kosher Sausage Corp., 2900 W. Devon.) Selma and her brother Ben Gerson have been dispensing

homemade chopped liver and the ubiquitous kosher corned beef at this
location for more than 21 years. Soups include matzo, kreplach, barley,
vegetable and split pea. AM 2-7391.

S & S Deli (aka Goldie's Pump Room)
694 Roger Williams
Highland Park   432-0775

Mildred and Aaron Goldstein run the S & S Deli, 694 Roger Williams,
Highland Park, (aka Goldie's Pump Room, local joke) in this North
Shore suburb, and their personal touch creates a warm ambiance.
There's a little bit of everything here, such as a grocery and candy store,
but the deli seeker will lust for the corned beef sandwiches manufactured by himself. Goldie adds that touch of class that transforms a mere
purchase into an experience. The Goldsteins open up at 6 a.m. Monday
through Friday and close at 8 p.m. On Saturday they're open from 6
a.m. to 7:30 p.m. and on Sunday from 6 a.m. to 7 p.m. 432-0755.

Al's Deli
18677 Dixie Highway
Homewood   SY 8-4399

Unlike Chicago's north suburbs, the Second City's southern boonies
might be described as deli-starved. A notable exception is Al's Deli at
18677 Dixie Highway in Homewood.
    Owners Al Laks and Wally Ginsberg cook their own corned beef and
hand-cut their lox. All soups are homemade, and the cabbage soup is
especially recommended.
    Also home-made are the potato latkes and strudel. Al's does a big
breakfast business, with lox omelettes a specialty.
    Al's is a *hamische* place that draws deli aficionados from the wilds of
northwest Indiana and as far south as Kankakee. Nearby Washington
Park racetrack sends its denizens and major league ballplayers and

umpires (noted gourmets all) have been in attendance, as has Muhammad Ali.

Al is in charge of the walls. His eclectic decor ranges from mounted fish through a Yiddish eye chart to Mona Lisa noting that "it wouldn't hurt."

The owners (Wally is a *schreier*), the walls, the employees and the customers add up to a sort of south-of-Chicago Runyonesque atmosphere.

Products are strictly kosher. Beer available. Lazy Susans, dairy and meat party platters to go. Open 6:30 to 7, seven days a week. SY 8-4399. Parting words from Wally and Al: "If you don't smell it, we don't sell it."

Armanetti
5425 S. LaGrange Rd.
Countryside   FL 4-0355
4151 W. Dundee Rd.
Northbrook   564-1040

If you want strictly kosher from Armanetti, the north side location (4151 W. Dundee, Northbrook) has more offerings. But if you want a wider variety — especially cheeses — then the southwest location (5425 S. LaGrange Rd., Countryside— is better. Try sniffing the 24-foot-long dairy tray with imported cheeses from all over the world. And the wine selection is equally assorted. For a particular treat, try the sausage. It's made on the premises. And on special occasions such as Columbus Day, the television cameras always seem to find Frank Armanetti, the family head, carrying on an old custom, grinding the sausage himself. Both delis are open from 9 a.m. to 10 p.m. weekdays and from 10 a.m. to 7 p.m. Sundays. FL 4-0355, 564-1040.

Sam & Hy's Delicatessen
3438 Dempster Street
Skokie   OR 4-8560

Sam & Hy's started out on Roosevelt Road in Chicago 29 years ago and
has been in Skokie (at 3438 Dempster Street) for the last 22 years.

It gets its name in the local papers quite often, especially because of
the visiting celebrities from nearby Mill Run theater. Some of the things
they like are the broiled Jewish liver, chicken in the pot, boiled beef
and braised short ribs.

There are homemade soups, but no liquor. Hours are 5:30 a.m. to
12:45 a.m. (until 1:45 a.m. Saturdays). Closed Rosh Hashanah, Yom
Kippur and in the daytime on Christmas and New Year's. OR 4-8560.

INDIANA

Shapiro's Delicatessen-Cafeteria
808 South Meridian
Indianapolis   631-4041

Shapiro's Delicatessen-Cafeteria, 808 South Meridian, Indianapolis, is the
healthy progeny of a grocery business that was started in 1905 by the
father of Max Shapiro, the current proprietor.

Everything at Shapiro's is homemade. Hot lunches and dinners include corned beef and cabbage, stuffed cabbage, brisket, and even a
kosher Irish stew.

All the old favorites are on display: corned beef, pastrami, frankfurters, tongue, and salami sandwiches are just a few. And don't forget to
eat your vegetables — they're fresh. You can also have fresh fruits with
sour cream, or homemade cheesecake.

There's a take-out counter, and beer is served. Shapiro's is open from
6:45 a.m. until 7:45 p.m. daily, except legal holidays. 631-4041.

IOWA

Dave Bassman's Manhattan Delicatessen
3705 Ingersoll
Des Moines   274-1208

Des Moines is the capital of Iowa. The capitol building has a gold dome. As when passing the gold dome of Notre Dame in Indiana, you can see the Iowa capitol from Interstate 80. If you want to visit the capitol, OK, but there's also Dave Bassman's Manhattan Delicatessen at 3705 Ingersoll.

Dave is reputed to have the best selection of cheeses in town, including *real* Roquefort, Gorgonzola, Reblochon, and the like. In addition, he has "Dave's Special" — corned beef and Swiss on a heated onion roll. Dave also serves his own chopped liver. (That's made from chickens, not his own liver chopped.) Among the other offerings are homemade matzo ball soup and cheesecake, plus a full selection of baked goods, including bagels.

Dave's place is eat-in and take-out. Beer to go only. It's open from 8 - 6, except Sundays and Jewish holidays. 274-1208.

Fishel's Deli
1215 Merle Hay Mall
Des Moines   276-9126

Even if you have nothing else to shop for in Des Moines, it's worth a trip to the Merle Hay Mall at the northwest edge of the city to visit Fishel's Deli. (No. 1215 in the mall.)

Hot off the grill is Fishel's "Official Special" — a combination of pastrami, turkey, sauerkraut and cheddar. You'd expect other big sellers like corned beef and Reubens, of course, but Fishel's also serves a variety of Poor Boys (or you can call them hoagies or subs.)

Good cheese selection, too. And Fishel's must be doing something right — you can have beer on the premises.

You can eat there or take it away from 10 - 9 Monday through Friday; 10 - 5:30 Saturday, and 11 - 5:30 Sunday. 276-9126.

Rapaport's Delicatessen
6935 Douglas
Des Moines   278-8931

You're still in Iowa? Don't leave Des Moines yet. However, I empathize with the urge. You've flatlanded it across Ohio, Indiana, Illinois, Iowa, (Nebraska is yet to come) and you yearn for the mountains of Wyoming. First, you'll eat.

You could try Rapaport's Delicatessen at 6935 Douglas. The local restaurant maven has described its pastrami sandwiches as "wonderful" and its onion rolls as "magnificent." Mike Rapaport adds that the No. 1 seller is his Reuben.

There are also bagels and lox and other sandwiches, including corned beef and roast beef. You can eat in or take it out. Again, beer to go only. (It's some kind of strange Iowa law having to do with the presence or absence of non-co-ed johns.)

Rapaport's is open from 7 - 7:30 Monday-Friday; 'til 7 on Saturday, and closed Sunday. 278-8931.

KANSAS   (see Missouri)

KENTUCKY

Brown and Bentley Cheese and Francy Foods Company
1324 E. Washington St.
Louisville   587-7036

Brown and Bentley Cheese and Fancy Foods Company is one of the shops in Bakery Square in Butchertown, one of Louisville's oldest neighborhoods (1324 East Washington Street.)

Bakery Square itself is a converted old bakery, now comprising a variety of shops. Brown and Bentley features imported cheeses, and such things as sassafras tea and grind-it-yourself peanut butter. Light lunches include "downhome" deserts. Surroundings are turn-of-the-century country store. 587-7036.

Kienle's German Delicatessen and Restaurant
Shelbyville Road Plaza
Louisville   897-3920

Kienle's German Delicatessen and Restaurant is located in Louisville's Shelbyville Road Plaza. It features German meats, sausages, breads and cheeses.
Kienle's has carry-outs and does catering. Open from 10 - 9, Tuesday through Saturday. Dinner served 6 - 9. 897-3920.

Les and Mark's Deli Place
2220 Hikes Lane
Louisville   456-4650

Next time you're at the Derby and develop a craving for something other than horseflesh, our Louisville deli maven suggests that you might want to try some of the following establishments in his area.
Les and Mark's Deli Place, 2220 Hikes Lane, opened recently, but reportedly has been so successful that another operation is planned in the east end of Louisville. The new place will seat about 100 and will do its own baking, including bagels.
Currently, Les and Mark's lists a roster of 40 combination sandwiches, plus "regular" and open-faced sandwiches. Hot dinner and brunch specials are offered, along with homemade soups and side dishes.
Other homemade specials include knishes, noodle pudding and chopped liver. Catering is another specialty and take-outs are available. (One of their ads suggests calling in advance — "No more Bicentennial Service . . . no more 200 years waiting for service.") Open seven days. 456-4650.

The Delikatessen and Restaurant
2222 Dundee Rd.
Louisville   452-1707

At 2222 Dundee Road is The Delikatessen and Restaurant, where the accent, as you can tell by the spelling, is German.
Try the *Kalter Aufschnitt, Kase Teller,* or *Der Feldmarschall.* (Cold cut plate, cheese plate and ham, cheese and BLT.) Several *wurst* sandwiches are offered, plus corned beef, pastrami and other standards. Homemade soups and salads, also beer. Carry-outs and catering. 452-1707.

MASSACHUSETTS

Kens
549 Boylston St.
Boston   CO 6-6149, 6106, 6150

The land of the bean and the cod is also the home of the bagel and schrod, among other viands aqueous and otherwise. The place for deli variety and volume in Boston is Kens at Copley, 549 Boylston Street. By virtue of its four-story building, Kens qualifies as the world's largest delicatessen. The 275-seat restaurant and take-out counter are on the first floor, and the rest of the building is devoted to food preparation. Everything is homemade including the bagels (plain, raisin, garlic, egg and pumpernickel.)

Kens pickles its own corned beef, and will even bake you a wedding cake if you are so inclined. The home-baked pastries can only be described as mouth-watering, and I do not use that term loosely. Night Manager Joel Cohen says the pastries are low-cal: "Every bite in the low thousands." (Kens recently was a second-place winner in National Restaurant Association competition.)

Kens serves 3,000 people a day, and waiting lines are not unusual. Waiting customers are often treated to hot tea and salami, which is especially good when it's raining.

One of the rambling menu's many features is "Sandwiches," but that's followed by "More Sandwiches." For example, you can get a pastrami sandwich, an overstuffed pastrami sandwich, or if that's not big enough, a huge pastrami sandwich. You can also order your pastrami sandwich served in combination with just about anything, provided you're willing to take a chance on the possibility of a synergistic reaction. Or try the Penn Special: Hot corned beef between two potato pancakes with sweet red pepper. There are also eggs, salads, burgers, cold platters, knishes, blintzes, onward and upward to a one-pound New York cut sirloin.

Wash it all down with a pitcher of cocktails, wine, or beer. If you're the nostalgic type, the fountain features a 2c plain ... for five cents. Kens draws show biz people, sports figures, and pols, including the Kennedys, we're told. Joel says the place is particularly lively between 2 and 3 a.m. He should know; he's the night manager. Kens is open from 7 a.m. 'til 3 a.m. 363 days a year. Closed Thanksgiving and Christmas. There are three other Kens, but this is the biggie. Party platters available. CO 6-6149, 6106, 6150.

Guenther and Handel
1558 Main Street
Springfield   737-4379

About three years ago, Guenther and Handel moved to its present location at 1558 Main Street in downtown Springfield, Massachusetts. It's now going on 74 years old.

G & H formerly was a gourmet shop, but now serves breakfast, lunch and dinner in addition to carry-outs. The ambiance is Germanic. Knockwurst and kraut is a big favorite.

There's also a good selection of other hot meals and sandwiches. Salads are homemade, with German potato salad a best seller. Beer and wine are served, and catering is offered.

Manager June Schunk says that G & H is now serving its third generation of customers and that there is an area-wide awareness of G & H throughout the Northeast by German-Americans and transplanted Springfielders.

Hours are 7 a.m. until 7 p.m. Monday through Saturday. Closed Sundays and all national holidays. 737-4379.

MICHIGAN

Samuels Brothers Cafeteria
2493 Russell
Detroit   WO 3-9199

Pretend it's like it used to be. You wanna buy a live chicken, you can get one at Detroit's Eastern Market. Even if you don't want a live chicken, across the street, at 2493 Russell, you'll find Samuels Brothers Cafeteria.

Don't let the "cafeteria" name bother you — it's a deli like you won't find in downtown Detroit anymore. (It's actually about three minutes from downtown, according to owner Morris Samuels.) Morris started out there in 1927, and he's still going strong, assisted by his son Ira.

The hours are somewhat unusual because of the adjoining market. It's the only deli I've encountered that *opens* at 3 a.m. But enjoy. Have chopped and fried eggplant, cheese blintzes and fresh fruit, brisket, boiled beef flanken, chicken (not live), turkey, lamb shanks, baked short ribs. Fresher everything couldn't be because the market is across the street.

Not enough? If you want a sandwich, buy one — any kind. Also fish and chopped liver. If you have a thing for baked goods, Samuels does its own, including bagels. You can also have beer and wine.

To appreciate the marketplace ambiance, you should be there on weekends, when anywhere from 2,000 to 3,000 people eat at Samuels Brothers. Why should they come then? I'll tell you.

Detroit's Eastern Market is the traditional farmers' market whereinto the farmers bring their agricultural wares (including live chickens.) During the week it's mostly commercial, but on weekends people from Motown do their shopping there. It's still kind of a funky place, with buildings dating from the early 1900's. It's been revamped to some extent, but not remodeled, except for a pop art paint job.

That horrendous opening hour, as I said, is 3 a.m. Closing time is 3:45 p.m. (Sort of like Les Halles in Paris used to be.) It's closed Sundays and national holidays. WO 3-9199.

Stage Deli
13821 West Nine Mile Road
Oak Park   LI 8-1111

Far from the madding crowd of Detroit's Eastern Market, the Stage Deli offers hot, fresh imported rye bread (from Detroit) in the close-in suburb of Oak Park at 13821 West Nine Mile Road.

You can have all the deli staples on that famous rye, or select a complete dinner. Included are steaks, fish, chicken and brisket.

Also prominent are homemade gefilte fish, bagels and lox, blintzes, chopped liver and potato pancakes. Eat in or take it out, but no beer or wine.

In keeping with its name, the Stage has a celeb-style decor. Show biz types don't drop by in person much anymore, because a nearby play-house has closed down. However, the memories linger on as the stars of yore keep the Stage's proprietors advised of their progress in greener pastures (or other revivals.)

The house lights go down on Mondays and on Thanksgiving. Other-wise, the Stage is open from 11 a.m. 'til 9 p.m. Tuesday through Sunday. LI 8-1111.

MINNESOTA

Emily's Lebanese Deli
641 University Ave., N.E.
Minneapolis   336-1416

If you're not Lebanese, there are some pretty exotic names listed on the menu at Emily's Lebanese Deli, 641 University Avenue, N.E. in Minnea-polis. Translated, however, they spell "delicious."

Take kibby, for instance. You can have it raw, baked, a combination of both, fried in a sandwich, or as a side order. Depending upon the variation ordered, it's beef or beef and lamb, with cracked wheat and seasonings.

Also among the daily specials and combination dinners are cabbage rolls, meat pies, and stuffed zucchini. Shish Kabob, of course, plus barbecued kafta (beef and seasonings.) And then there's lubin (yogurt) with grape leaves. All such orders include tabooley salad and Lebanese flat bread.

(Tabooley salad, also available as a side dish, contains cracked wheat, onions, tomatoes, parsley, and seasonings.) Also listed among the side orders are spinach pie and meat pie; ripe and green olives with feta cheese, and dips (with flat bread) — homos bitahini, (chick pea) lubin, and egg plant.

Turkish coffee appears among the beverages, but no alcohol is served. For dessert, try baklawa (made with walnuts and a special sugar syrup), or the shumboosak cookie.

Emily's is open from 9 - 8:30 (until 9:30 on weekends), and closed Tuesdays. It's eat-in and take-out. 336-1416.

MISSOURI

**Protzel's Delicatessen
7608 Wydown Blvd.
Clayton   721-4445**

In the St. Louis suburb of Clayton, Bob Protzel, "the delicatessen bard," holds forth, intermittently slicing lox in the front and writing advertising copy and comedy material in the back room. The scene is Protzel's Delicatessen at 7608 Wydown Boulevard in Clayton.

Along with his gags, Bob says the following are his specialties: "Fresh, not frozen, hand-sliced lox (Nova and regular). We cook our own corned beef. Our own roast briskets, chopped liver, kasha varnishkes, knishes, mandle bread, snappy conversation, jokes (old, new, funny, and eh), honest weight, correct change, sincere 'please' and 'thank you,' a beautiful wife, and fresh-baked breads, rolls, and sweets delivered two or three times daily. We also make our own salads, and carry a complete line of cheeses."

Bob's deli is take-out only, but sometimes customers will eat sandwiches while standing at the counter (and listening to Bob). He does visuals, too, tacking up one-liners on the wall behind the counter. However, Bob's writing has made an impact far beyond Wydown Boulevard. His ads have appeared nationally in print and on TV and radio, and several well-known comics have bought his gags. When he heard one of his jokes on the air, Bob realized that some not-so-well known comics could steal his material, too. (For a sample of Bob's writing, see page 33.)

But back to the deli. Protzel's is open from 8 to 5:45 Tuesday through Sunday. It's closed Monday unless it's a national holiday. In that event, it's open a half day Monday and closed Tuesday. 721-4445.

Dinkeldorf's Deli and Dining
7084 W. 105th
Overland Park (Kansas)   341-4170

5249 Antioch Rd.
Kansas City   454-8100

Dinkledorf's Deli and Dining has two locations in the Kansas City area — one in Overland Park, Kansas; the other on the Missouri side. The Overland Park location is 7084 West 105th. In Kansas City, Missouri, it's 5249 Antioch Road.

The food mixture is eclectic. Among the offerings are knishes, escargot, bagels and lox, Japanese chicken, salami, and a selection of Greek foods.

If you don't want corned beef, pastrami, or a Reuben, try the vegetarian "Anti-Fatso." Other specialties are Crab Rangoon, black beans and rice, and gangplank flank steak.

Recommended especially for parties is the "Big Mother Hogie" — a five-foot sandwich with 14 ingredients. It's also sold by the inch or by the foot. Or try a rainbow burger — served on an English muffin with cheddar, bacon and avocado.

There's an omelette bar where you can pick your own ingredients. (All day in Missouri, after 10 p.m. in Kansas.) In the Missouri establishment there's a spud bar where you have your choice of ingredients served in a large, fluffy mashed potato.

Dinkledorf's is open seven days a week: From 10 'til 3 a.m. and 'til 4 on weekends. (At this writing, the Kansas location is in the process of becoming a 24-hour operation.) Closed Christmas in the daytime. Carry-out and catering available. Beer only in Kansas, full bar in Missouri. Entertainment after midnight in both places. 341-4170 (Overland Park), 454-8100 (Kansas City.)

New York Bakery and Delicatessen
7016 Troost Ave.
Kansas City   523-0432

The New York Bakery & Delicatessen, 7016 Troost Avenue, Kansas City, has been in business 60 years and is currently operated by the third generation of the Becker family, who describe their establishment as "A friendly place to meet and eat."

All its breads, pastries and bagels are homemade. Best sellers are corned beef and pastrami sandwiches. (Meats are cooked on the premises.)

There are other sandwiches, chopped liver, salads and knishes. Carryouts and party trays are available.

The NYB & D is open from 7 a.m. 'til midnight seven days a week. Closed Jewish holidays. 523-0432.

O'Riley's Pumpernickel Deli
117 E. 12th St.
Kansas City   421-2230

Perhaps only in America could it be named O'Riley's Pumpernickel Deli. It's at 117 East 12th Street in downtown Kansas City.

O'Riley's features sandwiches such as meat ball and sausage grinders, corned beef, pastrami and bagels and lox.

It's open from 8 to 6, six days. Closed Sundays and holidays. No alcohol. 421-2230.

Paul's Main Street Delicatessen
5044 Main
Kansas City   753-9345

Just off Kansas City's plaza is Paul's Main Street Delicatessen at 5044 Main. The business goes back 60 years and it has been under its current ownership for the last 14.

Paul's serves corned beef, lox, salami and the other old favorites, plus homemade salads and beer. It's open from 8 - 9 Monday through Thursday, 8 - 11 Friday, and 8 - 10 Saturday. Closed Sundays and holidays. 753-9345.

MONTANA

Bert & Ernie's Last Chance Saloon & Delicatessen
415 N. Main St.
Helena   443-9750

It may be your last chance in Montana, so stop at Bert & Ernie's Last Chance Saloon & Delicatessen at 415 North Main Street in Helena. (If you want more atmosphere, Main Street is also known as Last Chance Gulch.)

Bert & Ernie's serves a good selection of cold meat and cheese sandwiches, salads, chili, and homemade soups. (Two of the favorites are borscht and ham hock and bean.) You can eat in or take it away on horseback. Beer and wine are available.

The striking decor features rustic barnwood, stained glass, log booths, and brick and rock walls. Bert & Ernie's is open from 11 - 9 weekdays; 9 - midnight on Saturdays, and closed Sundays and major holidays. 443-9750.

NEBRASKA

Leon's Food Mart
2200 Winthrop Rd.
Lincoln   488-2307

Leon's Food Mart is a take-out establishment at 2200 Winthrop Road (at 32nd and South) in Lincoln, Nebraska, home of the Cornhusker State's famous skyscraper capitol.

It has kosher-style standard sandwiches, hot foods and cold salads, bagels and lox, cheeses, Reubens, fried and barbecued chicken, and barbecued ribs.

Leon's bills itself as "The Stage Door Deli" because of its theatrical decor. In keeping with that motif, its catering services are handled by the "Deli Dollies."

Hours are 8:30 a.m. - 6:30 p.m., except for Thursday and Friday, when it's open until 8:30 p.m. Closed Sundays and holidays. No beer or wine. 488-2307.

My Mama's Delicatessen
1321 Jones St.
Omaha   342-6262

My Mama's Delicatessen, at 1321 Jones Street in downtown Omaha, is a new place that incorporates old Omaha decor in an equally old building.

Don't get lost. You enter just off a loading dock. Inside, the current big sellers are pastrami and corned beef among the longtime deli favorites. Bagels and lox also are featured, and as of this writing, plans are under way to serve blintzes and soups.

You can wash down your cheesecake with natural fruit-flavored Tehuacan carbonated mineral water imported from Mexico. Also on the fountain menu: Old-fashioned malts, phosphates, and egg cream. There's no beer or wine, but you can have Bierell near-beer from Switzerland. Manager Cindy Williams says it contains only seven calories per bottle yet tastes like imported dark beer. Cindy and her boss are responsible for the decor, reportedly the envy of professional decorators.

The interior features hand-hewn wood decor and old tables from Omaha's city hall. Candies are sold from an old Creighton University dental school counter. Who said we should avoid between-meal treats? But there is something new: My Mama's Yiddish radio commercials are on Omaha's Hit Parade.

My Mama's has a specialty food shop, and also sells plants and Mexican lighting fixtures. Hours are 11 - 8 Monday through Friday, 'til 10 on Saturday. (The shop opens an hour earlier.) Sunday hours are 12 - 4. 342-6262.

NEVADA

Peppina's New Delicatessen Market
4813 Paradise Rd.   **2215 E. Lake Mead**
Las Vegas   **North Las Vegas   736-0531**

If you have to eat while gambling in Las Vegas, Peppina's New Delicatessen Market offers variety. It's located at 4813 Paradise Road, with a branch at 2215 East Lake Mead in North Las Vegas.

Peppina's specializes in Italian and Greek foods, plus representative items from other ethnic sources. More than 50 varieties of cheese are in stock, as well as 44 different kinds of meat. Eat in or take out.

Featured are homemade sausage, meat balls, roasts, and sauces. Beer and wine are available.

Peppina's is open from 9 to 10, seven days a week. Closed Christmas, New Year's, Easter, and Thanksgiving. 736-0531.

NEW MEXICO

Franchini Brothers Grocery and Delicatessen
1800 Lomas Blvd., N.E.
Albuquerque 243-1757

Franchini Brothers Grocery and Delicatessen, 1800 Lomas Boulevard N.E. in Albuquerque, is a large, bright, take-out establishment that features Italian, Greek, and Arabic specialties.

In addition to groceries and meats, Franchini's has a full liquor store, sandwiches to go, and does catering.

It's open 8 to 7, six days a week. (Closed Sundays.) 243-1757

Mark's International Restaurant and Delicatessen
105 Stanford Dr., S.E.
Albuquerque 268-4789

Mark's International Restaurant and Delicatessen, 105 Stanford Drive S.E., Albuquerque, features an almost infinite variety of elaborate double and triple submarine sandwiches.

And there's more, much more, like brisket, homemade soups and salads, blintzes, knishes, bagels and lox, and chopped liver without mayonnaise.

In keeping with its international name, Mark's also offers Mexican, Chinese, Italian, and German dishes. Owner Sid, a transplanted New Jerseyite, says that tongue doesn't go over in Albuquerque, and that herring has only a so-so reception. However, Mark's top-of-the-line item, a large, reasonably priced T-bone, goes over very well.

Mark's is located in an attractive old house near the University of New Mexico campus. There's a dining room, sun porch, and an outdoor patio. Take-out also.

Hours are 7 to 10 Monday through Friday, 10 'til 10 Saturday, and closed Sunday. 268-4789.

The Winery
Galisteo and Water
Santa Fe 988-2984

A couple of blocks from the historic Santa Fe Plaza is an attractive establishment, The Winery, at Galisteo and Water. High adobe walls, brick floors, and rough-hewn aged lumber set a southwestern atmosphere.

Its bar and deli section specializes in smoked beef and pastrami sandwiches served with half-sour kosher pickles. It serves a full line of imported beers, with emphasis on the Mexican brands.

The Winery stocks more than 600 varieties of imported and domestic wines, 100 cheeses, 35 kinds of whole bean coffee, gourmet foods, and accessories.

According to owner Richard Heller, until The Winery opened three years ago, such specialties as fillo pastry leaves, falafel, Syrian bread, and Nova were unavailable in Santa Fe. 988-2984.

NEW YORK

2nd Avenue Delicatessen-Restaurant
156 2nd Ave.
New York   AL 4-7144

Could it be that you've only been to Second Avenue while listening to Barbra Streisand? Forget the fantasy and enjoy the real thing. Stop at the corner of 10th Street and Second, and visit the 2nd Avenue Delicatessen-Restaurant, 156 Second Avenue. (Strictly kosher.)

Be prepared to be fed. For instance, if you're in a party of three or four, you can order the "Open Sandwich Medley." You get corned beef, tongue, roast beef, turkey, pastrami, chopped liver, eggs and mushrooms, salami, and potato salad.

There's also a special kettle of soup that serves three. Or if you're by yourself, you can order half a sandwich and a plate of soup. The sandwich selection is rampant. There are three deckers, hot open-faced, and just plain sandwiches. Example: roast turkey and breast of beef with chicken fat, onion, cole slaw, and Russian dressing. You can also get a lettuce and tomato if you're on some kind of weird diet.

You'd rather have fish? Have tuna, salmon, sardines, gefilte, filet of sole, baked carp or whitefish. Lox, too, of course.

Complete dinners are served from 5 to 9 p.m. At the top of the entree list is chicken in the pot made with noodles, vegetables, and matzo ball. For the same price you can have boiled beef in the pot with the same accompaniment.

Also available: meatball, derma, and stuffed cabbage combination; a whole pound of boiled beef flanken; potted breast of beef; corned beef and cabbage; steaks, and more.

Beer (including Israeli) and ale are served. Non-alcoholic beverages include birch beer (long time no see), and you can order a family-style

pitcher of soda (pop to Midwesterners). Breakfast specials and catering, too.
The 2nd Avenue is open from 7 a.m. to midnight, seven days a week. Closed Passover, Rosh Hashanah, and Yom Kippur. AL 4-7144.

Fine & Schapiro's
138 W. 72nd St.
New York   TR 7-2874

If you like *pucha,* and who doesn't, Fine & Schapiro's, 138 West 72nd Street, is the place to go. The 49-year-old establishment near Upper Broadway is noted for its old Jewish delicacies not generally available. Such as *pucha,* which, as you know, is frozen calves' feet.
The huge menu is kosher catholic, even including a couple of Chinese dishes. A few of the entrees are lamb stew, fried kreplach, stuffed kishka, boiled beef flanken, Hungarian beef goulash, and broiled Roumanian tenderloin steak.
Beer and wine (domestic, Israeli, and French) are served. Party platters and complete take-out service available, featuring fruit-decorated carved turkeys. Open 8:30 a.m. - 11:30 p.m. except Friday, when closing time is 9 p.m. Closed during the high holidays. Strictly kosher, but open Saturdays. F & S attracts its quota of show biz and political types, too. Recent visitors include the ever-popular Shelley Winters and Senator Jake Javits. We do *not* know if they were at the same table. To find out, call TR 7-2874.

Katz's
205 E. Houston St.
New York   AL 4-2246

Hop a southbound subway and head for 205 East Houston Street. (If you're not indigenous to the Apple, remember not to pronounce it like the city in Texas. In New York, it's "How"-ston.) Anyway, there at Houston and Ludlow is a rambling ranch of a deli — Katz's.
According to salami lovers everywhere, Katz's opening was the other major event back in '88 (in addition to The Blizzard). Signs abound behind the seemingly mile-long counter. That's where you'll find the prices. There are none on the menu, which is a sign of the times. Staying on a sign kick, be sure to check the big one hanging from the ceiling. It proclaims the famed slogan of a World War II owner: "Send a Salami to Your Boy in the Army." In New York, that rhymes.
Enough signs. Let's get down to why you're here. You can make

your selection cafeteria-style or live it up with a venerable waiter. Katz's cures its own meats and serves the usual spectrum. If you like garlic, a specialty is "Knobel" Wurst. You can have your meat mounded on a sandwich or draped on a platter, with or without eggs, salads, or assorted side dishes. Beer and soft drinks are available, including the ever-popular Dr. Brown's Cel-Ray Tonic. Or try a glass of tea. Plump frankfurters are loaded with mustard and sauerkraut. If you don't like mustard and sauerkraut, they'll probably sell you a plain hot dog, but Izzy the manager undoubtedly will regard you as some kind of freak.

Catering and party platters available. Open from 7 a.m. to midnight, 'til 2 a.m. on Fridays and Saturdays. Izzy recommends salamis as business gifts. Says they're better than booze. AL 4-2246.

Paprikas Weiss Importer
1546 2nd Ave.
New York   288-6903

Only part of Paprikas Weiss Importer at 1546 Second Avenue may be considered a take-out deli. The store is loaded with foods, cookware, books, gifts and other items, and does a huge mail order business. The two big deli-type goodies are homemade Hungarian salami and sausage. Ed Weiss, third generation proprietor of the business, which has been around for 85 years, notes that the sausage has been brought along on Himalayan and other mountain-climbing expeditions. Its nutritional value is reportedly highly concentrated, and it's compact.

The Hungarian salami, made according to an old secret family recipe, is recommended by famed gourmet Clementine Paddleford!

In addition to its own paprika and a myriad of other spices, the store's catalogue is extensive. You can find all sorts of food, exotic and otherwise, coffees, teas, cheeses, candies and pastries, cookware, utensils, Paprikas' own Hungarian cookbook, peasant blouses, dolls, goosefeather pastry brushes, and on and on. (Catalogue is published four times a year — annual subscription $1.)

Paprikas Weiss is open six days from 9 to 6. 288-6903.

Ratner's
138 Delancey St.
New York   677-5588

Although Ratner's, at 138 Delancey Street, is a dairy restaurant and not a deli, tradition demands that it be included herein.

A new York institution since 1918, Ratner's always reminded me of what in my imagination the dining salon of a luxury liner looked like in the early days of steam.

In a more practical vein, its overflowing baskets of bagels, bialys and onion rolls helped me through NYU.

Now that you can afford more than the rolls and coffee, try the mushroom steak or roast, or the vegetable liver salad.

Ratner's has all kinds fish and blintzes, too — in fact almost anything you want — as long as it's meatless.

Catering, platters, and take-out services. Open 6-12 seven days a week. 677-5588.

Stage Delicatessen
834 7th Ave.
New York   CI 5-7850

The Big Apple is also Queen City of the Deli ... It's got to be where it all began. (Legend has it that Peter Stuyvesant was a corned beef-and-Swiss man.) Two of Manhattan's 1,980 Yellow Pages are jammed full of deli listings. Let your fingers do the walking and stop in the S's ... Specifically, the Stage Delicatessen at 834 Seventh Avenue.

Long-renowned not only for its food but also for its celebrity-viewing, the Stage is the ultimate adornment in the Queen City's diadem.

Deli aficionados who haven't been there in a year or so are in for a bit of a shock. The plain decor of yore has been replaced by rather sumptuous new surroundings.

Genial owner Jim Richter assures his fans out there that only the atmosphere has changed, that it's still the same good food with more comfort.

Two of the outstanding new features are a bar (formerly only beer was available) and a sidewalk cafe. Don't fret about the Seventh Avenue bus fumes, though. The cafe is glass-enclosed. Adding to the ambiance are the brass railings from the late lamented Roxy Theater surrounding the bar. (It's a good-sized watering hole, but Jim insists that it's "intimate." Probably depends on your drinking partner.) Along with the new decor came additional seating. Capacity has been increased to 135 from 84.

The menu is long and complete, including a moderately priced wine list, but this is the heart of the matter, this is what keeps 'em coming back:

STAGE SPECIALTIES

STAGE SPECIAL: Three Decker Sandwich with Corned Beef, Tongue and Swiss Cheese, Russian Dressing, Cole Slaw

HOWIE SPECIAL: Open Sliced Corned Beef or Pastrami, Melted Cheese and Hot Sauerkraut

JIMMY'S SPECIAL: Three Decker Sandwich, Corned Beef, Pastrami, Swiss Cheese, Cole Slaw, Russian Dressing

MAX'S SPECIAL: Three Decker Sandwich with Sliced Turkey, Tongue, Corned Beef, Russian Dressing, Cole Slaw

LOUIE SPECIAL: Three Decker Sandwich with Chopped Liver, Corned Beef, Tomato and Bermuda Onion

ARTIE SPECIAL: Three Decker Sandwich, Tongue, Hot Pastrami, Chicken Salami, Russian Dressing, Cole Slaw

BERNIE SPECIAL: Three Decker Sandwich with Genuine Lake Sturgeon, Nova Scotia Salmon, Lettuce and Tomato, Bermuda Onion

CELEBRITY SPECIAL: Three Decker Sandwich with Corned Beef, Pastrami, Chopped Liver and Onion

Open from 7 a.m. to 3 a.m. 365 days, but check first on Yom Kippur: CI 5-7850.

The Bremen House
200 E. 86th St.   **58-22 Myrtle Ave.**
New York   **Ridgewood   288-5500**

The Bremen House, 200 East 86th Street, is a bastion of New York's
Yorkville (German) section. There is also a branch at 58-22 Myrtle
Avenue in Ridgewood.

The Bremen House features more than 60 kinds of sausage, homemade salads, sandwiches, party platters, imported specialties, an organic
foods department, and many different cheeses.

Take-out only, the store does a large mail order business. Open 9-9
six days, 11-8 on Sunday. 288-5500.

Wish Bone's Deli
224 W. 79th St.
New York   877-7410

Up the street a ways, at 224 West 79th Street, is Wish Bone's Deli, only
a few months old. Enthusiastic young owner Frank Pipia specializes in
home cooking of Mediterranean food. All the usual deli goodies are on
display, but what catches the eye is the six-foot hero sandwich. If
you're not hungry, they're also available down to three feet. The bright
little store also manages to cram in gourmet and health food sections,
plus a variety of herbal teas. Open 9-11 Monday through Friday, and
9-9 on weekends. Take-out only. Catering service. 877-7410.

Zabar's
2245 Broadway
New York   787-2000

Zabar's, at 2245 Broadway, has to be seen — and smelled. This attrac-
tively cluttered urban barn might be described as a super-deli cum
continental general store. It's take-out only. Who could find a place to
sit? But such things you can take out:

More than 100 varieties of salami and sausage dangle from the rafters,
cheeses range from wheels to wedges, salads sing and fishes flaunt.

There are all kinds of bread to put the cheeses and sausages on, and
tons and tons of the goodies that always seem to be described as
"continental delicacies." (Also domestic.)

There's a swell-smelling section devoted to coffee and teas, and
enough cookware to feed the Israeli Army for at least six days.

Zabar's is open from 8 to 7:30 Sunday through Thursday; 'til 10 on
Friday, and 'til 12 on Saturday. 787-2000.

New York's Pastrami Olympics'

Back in 1973, the noted Underground Gourmet department of New York Magazine conducted a "Pastrami Olympics" among delis in the New York area.

Messengers (who gave their orders anonymously) rushed pastrami on rye with mustard and pickle from various establishments to a six-person jury gathered for the event.

The unidentified sandwiches were devoured and judged. Results appeared in the magazine and included a pastrami centerfold poster.

Some of the delis reviewed in this section were included, and others are listed below alphabetically. We're not going to give you the jury's ranking, because you know how things can change in three years.

One place in the Bronx appears to have disappeared in the interim. The others are in Manhattan, except Junior's, which is in Brooklyn. Where else would there be a Flatbush Avenue Extension?

P. J. Bernstein
1215 Third Avenue
879-0914

Carnegie
854 Seventh Avenue
PL 7-2245

Ershowsky
39 West 46th Street
247-5630

Gaiety West
224 West 47th Street
765-1240

Gitlitz
2183 Broadway
SU 7-2149

Harry & Ben's
225 West 47th Street
CI 5-8421

Henry's
195 East Houston Street
OR 4-2200

Hole in the Wall
1055 First Avenue
752-0540

Junior's
386 Flatbush Avenue Ext.
852-5257

Nathan's Famous
Broadway & 43rd Street
594-7455

Pastrami and Things
297 Third Avenue
683-7185

Regency
1311 Second Avenue
628-6200

Smokehouse
957 Third Avenue
421-4040

NORTH CAROLINA

Jay's Fine Foods
Friendly Shopping Center
Greensboro   292-0741

Sol Jacobs, owner of Jay's Fine Foods in the Friendly Shopping Center, Greensboro, North Carolina, says that his *real* specialty is "political advice."

However, he must be doing something else right, too. He has sold more than 600,000 of his nine-ingredient submarine sandwiches over the last 18 years. If you want something smaller, he'll oblige. Tell him his niece Harriet Marcus the newspaper columnist sent you. You can also have beer.

Jay's is open from 10 a.m. - 6 p.m. five days; until 9 p.m. on Fridays, and closed Sundays and national and Jewish holidays. 292-0741.

OHIO

Zenko's Olde World Deli
121 W. Indiana Ave.
Perrysburg   874-1401

Zenko's Olde World Deli, 121 West Indiana Avenue, Perrysburg, Ohio, is located in a Williamsburgish complex called Perry's Landing. (Perrysburg is just south of Toledo, near where Perry did his naval thing.)

Zenko's opened early in 1976 and has already attracted a lot of business. Three partners did all the interior decor, including butcher block tables on big black milk cans, and installation of ceiling fans.

Food is basically German and kosher. Twenty different kinds of meat were available the day of our visit, and sandwiches come in two sizes — large and huge, listed on the menu as regular and deluxe.

Also available: soups, potato salads, cheeses and desserts (try the millionaire pie). Soups, potato salads and some desserts are homemade. Everything can be ordered to go. Be careful of the oldenburger, though. It's not a venerable hamburger; it's onion-flavored liverwurst. Special meats and cheeses can be ordered. Party trays available.

Open 9-8 Monday through Thursday, until 10 on Friday and Saturday. Closed Sundays. 874-1401.

Warzy's Delicatessen & Wine Shop
3400 Glendale
Toledo   382-5656

Warzy's Delicatessen & Wine Shop, 3400 Glendale, Toledo, in the Southland shopping center, is take-out only.

Grinders and other sandwiches to go. Good selection of meats and cheeses. Seven varieties of bagels available on Fridays and Saturdays only.

Buy a bag of bagels and a jug of Chateau Lafite Rothschild '66 ($79.38) and live it up on the shores of beautiful Lake Erie.

Open 9 to 9, but never on Sunday. 382-5656.

Kravitz's Deli
3135 Belmont
Youngstown   759-7889

When you're in Youngstown (And why shouldn't you be? It's about half-way between New York and Chicago if you're driving or walking), you could try Kravitz's Deli at 3135 Belmont.

Specialties include deli submarines, a "Mighty Reuben," Hungarian kipfel, homemade soups, corned beef, pastrami, lox, herring, smoked fish, salami, and homemade bagels.

Eat in, or take it out. (Beer and wine to go only.) Kravitz's now seats 50 people and contains a bakery and carry-out section. Back in 1939, though, Mr. and Mrs. Kravitz started out in a 20 x 20-foot store at a different location in Youngstown. In those days pastries and bagels were imported from Cleveland.

Mrs. Rose Kravitz describes the atmosphere of her place as "noisy, friendly, but efficient." (Isn't that what a deli should be?) It's open from 9 - 9 seven days a week. 759-7889.

OKLAHOMA

Subway Deli
3323 Northwest Expressway
Oklahoma City   848-3621

The Subway Deli, 3323 Northwest Expressway, Oklahoma City, combines deli staples and other fare in colorful "country kitchen" surroundings.

If you're claustrophobic, fear not: The Subway Deli is not underground. On the level, it features 14 different sandwiches, including pastrami (kosher and extra lean), Reubens, subs, smoked ham and Swiss. (*Oklahoma Business* magazine says the Subway serves the best Reuben in the state.)

You can also get a rib eye, barbecue, soups, beer, frozen yogurt, and cheesecake. (The dessert line is being expanded.) If you want somebody to talk to, you can also buy a plant.

The Subway runs from 11 a.m. 'til 9 p.m. six days. It's off the track Sundays and national holidays. 848-3621.

Noshery
7011 South Memorial
Tulsa   252-5402

and

The Bagelry
5932 South Lewis
Tulsa   743-6770

The very new Noshery, 7011 South Memorial, Tulsa, is an offshoot of The Bagelry, a bakery and take-out and catering establishment at 5932 South Lewis, also in Tulsa. (Acclaimed by *Oklahoma Business* as one of the two places in the state offering the "Best Breakfast Buys.")

At the Noshery, located in a new shopping mall, you can eat in or take out menu items. They include traditional and open-faced sandwiches and hot meals. There are salad and soup bars, and desserts from The Bagelry. Among them, napoleons and eclairs.

According to owner Helene Laefer, a transplanted New Yorker, everything is made from scratch, including the knishes. Not homemade is the 3.2 beer that is served.

The Noshery is open Monday-Saturday from 9 a.m. until 8:30 p.m. Closed Thanksgiving, Christmas, and New Year's, but open Sundays during the holiday shopping season. 252-5402.

The Bagelry's hours are 9 a.m. - 8 p.m. Tuesdays through Fridays; 9 a.m. - 6 p.m. Saturdays, and 9 a.m. - 4 p.m. Sundays. Closed Thanksgiving, Christmas, New Year's, and Jewish holidays. 743-6770.

Gerti's Deli
5107 South Sheridan
Tulsa   664-5131

German specialties are featured at Gerti's Deli, 5107 South Sheridan, Tulsa, in keeping with its German decor.

Menu highlights are special German wursts, wieners, sauerkraut, potato salad, soups (including cheese, pea, lentil, and goulash), and pastries. Polish sausage, too. (*Oklahoma Business* rates Gerti's as the best German food in the state.)

Monday through Friday evenings special dinners are served — among them sauerbraten, roladen, wiener schnitzel, and pork rolls with red cabbage. Take-outs include German bread, meats, and cheeses. 3.2 beer is served.

Gerti's is open 10 a.m. to 8 p.m. from Monday to Friday, until 5 p.m. on Saturday. Closed holidays. By now a new downtown location should be open. 664-5131.

OREGON — Portland and area

Anderson's Delicatessen
9575 S.W. Beaverton Highway
Beaverton   643-5415

Anderson's Delicatessen, at 9575 S.W. Beaverton Highway in the Portland suburb of Beaverton, Oregon, serves sandwiches to eat in, or rather, eat out, only in the summer on its patio.

What makes it much more than a sandwich shop are the take-outs available year-round. Specialties are complete dinners, hot or frozen. Among the entrees are chicken curry, lasagna, stroganoff, and jambalaya. According to owner Vern Anderson, people from the hinterlands drop in to stock up their freezers and often spend $200 or more during the visit.

The accent is polyglot. Selection is Swedish, German, Swiss, French, English, Indian, Italian, Pakistani et al. Everything is home-cooked and home-baked. If you want, you can carry it away in one of the many baskets offered for sale.

Anderson's has a large wine (to go only) and cheese selection, and does catering. Seven fresh salads are featured daily, and there is fresh roasted coffee. It's located adjacent to metropolitan Portland, five minutes from downtown. Hours are 9 a.m. to 6 p.m. Monday through Saturday. Closed Sundays and major national holidays. 643-5415.

Goldberg's Delicatessen
1329 Lloyd Center
Portland   284-4004

Goldberg's Delicatessen, at 1329 Lloyd Center in downtown Portland, Oregon, dishes up its victuals in a fancy cafeteria style. You don't have to schlep your own tray. A busboy takes it to your table. Owner Richard Goldberg says that the service is fast, even when the crowds appear at lunchtime.

In addition to traditional sandwiches, which include Reubens, Goldberg's ladles a lot of borscht and features ribs at night. Baked goods are supplied by Goldberg's Kosher Bakery, which is under the same ownership. Draft beer is served.

Goldberg's opens at 11 a.m. and closes at 8 p.m. on Mondays and Thursdays; 7:30 p.m. on Tuesdays and Wednesdays; 8:30 p.m. on Fridays and 6 p.m. on Saturdays. It's closed Sundays and Christmas. 284-4004.

PENNSYLVANIA

Granny McGraw's Deli-Restaurant
1229 Chestnut St.
Philadelphia   564-2000

Granny McGraw's Deli-Restaurant in Philadelphia is not nearly as old as the Liberty Bell, since it was established in the year of the Bicentennial at 1229 Chestnut Street.

It's a large downtown establishment that employs a cafeteria-style set-up in an attractive Victorian decor. In addition to standard deli fare (including cooked-on-the-premises corned beef), it features freshly made salads (pick your own ingredients).

A beer license has been applied for, and take-out service is available.

Granny McGraw's is open from 11 - 7, six days a week. Closed Sundays
and major holidays, 564-2000.

Murray's Delicatessen
60th and Locust Sts.
Philadelphia   GR 2-9835

Murray's Delicatessen, at 60th and Locust Streets in West Philadelphia,
has been around for about 50 years. It serves sandwiches predominantly,
eat-in and take-out.

Murray's cooks its own corned beef, and serves beer. It's open from 8
- 6 Monday through Thursday; until 7:30 on Friday and Saturday, and
is open on Sunday from 11 until 4 or 5. Closed Yom Kippur. GR
2-9835.

R & W Delicatessen
128 S. 19th St.
Philadelphia   LO 3-7247

Also in downtown Philadelphia at 128 South 19th Street is the R & W
Delicatessen. Its menu features the old standby sandwiches, including
bagels and lox. Other breakfast items also are available.

The 18-year-old R & W is open from 9 - 12:30 a.m. seven days a
week. Closed Rosh Hashanah and Yom Kippur. Beer is served. LO
3-7247.

Iz Cohen's Delicatessen
2201 Murray Avenue
Pittsburgh   521-4555

By the time you read this, there probably still will be a 2201 Murray
Avenue in Pittsburgh, but Iz Cohen's name may have changed. The
premises are slated for expansion and bigger and better things are
expected, such as a family restaurant and banquet halls. Currently,
sandwiches (especially corned beef) and hot meals are available inside or
to go. Beer is served, but there may be a full bar in the offing. Hours
now are 7 a.m. to 1 a.m. seven days a week. Closed Rosh Hashanah and
Yom Kippur. 521-4555.

TENNESSEE

Zager's Deliteria
3716 Hillsboro Rd.
Nashville   297-7300

For Country & Western fans who are also deli devotees, there's Nashville, and in Nashville, Zager's Deliteria at 3716 Hillsboro Road.
Zager's specializes in sandwiches and catering, and does its own cooking and baking. You can eat in or take it out, and beer is available.
Open from 10 - 8 Monday through Friday; 10 - 6 Saturday, and 11 - 5 on Sunday. 297-7300.

TEXAS

Alfred's Restaurant, Delicatessen & Bakery
2408 Rice Boulevard   529-2891
9123 Stella Link Road   667-6541
520 Town & Country Village   464-5411
Houston

Alfred's has three locations in Houston — 2408 Rice Boulevard (near downtown and the medical center); 9123 Stella Link Road, and 520 Town & Country Village.
The food is basically kosher- and German-style with international overtones. Hot meals include corned beef and cabbage, sauerbraten, Hungarian stuffed cabbage, and baked chicken with dressing.
You can have regular or combo sandwiches, homemade soups, lox, kishka, home-baked breads and fancy desserts. Beer and wine, too. There are delicacy-type foods to go, plus deli meats, cheeses, party trays and catering. Gift baskets during the holidays.
The Rice Boulevard branch is open from 9 a.m. until 10 p.m. The other two locations from 8 a.m. until midnight. All are open seven days a week, except Christmas, New Year's, Rosh Hashanah and Yom Kippur. Phones are: 529-2891 (Rice Boulevard): 667-6541 (Stella Link), and 464-5411 (Town & Country).

UTAH

Marianne's Delicatessen
149 West 2nd South
Salt Lake City   364-0513

Especially for Rhinestein Cowboys in the intermountain region, the accent is Germanic at Marianne's Delicatessen, 149 West 2nd South in Salt Lake City.

Hot and cold sandwiches are served from noon until 2 p.m. Tuesday through Saturday. Among them are knockwurst, bratwurst, Polish sausage, and wieners. German imports and Usinger's sausages imported from Milwaukee are available, too. Breakfast is in the coffee-and-doughnuts genre, and there's no beer or wine at any time.

Take-outs include not only food, but also German magazines. Although I suppose if you want to read *Der Spiegel* while noshing on knockwurst, it would be permitted.

Marianne's is open from 9 a.m. - 6 p.m. five days. Closed Sundays, Mondays, and holidays. 364-0513.

VIRGINIA

Boulevard Delicatessen
5218 West Broad Street
Richmond   282-9333

Fat Yankees and overweight residents of the Old Dominion alike might want to try some of the deli-type Weight Watchers specials served at the Boulevard Delicatessen, 5218 West Broad Street, Richmond.

Those without weight problems might prefer Reubens and other sandwiches, hot meals that include brisket and steaks, or bagels and lox. Salads and a large fish selection (such as kippers, sable, chubs) also are available, as are beer and wine. Omelettes are a biggie at breakfast time.

To-go item also include candies, fruit baskets, champagnes, and gifts from Israel. Catering, too. Open Sunday through Thursday from 9 a.m. until 7:45 p.m.; until 9 p.m. on Friday and Saturday. 282-9333.

WASHINGTON

Mama Reuben's Bakery, Delicatessen & Restaurant
7660 S.E. 27th
Mercer Island   232-4000

Mama Reuben's, at 7760 S.E. 27th, Mercer Island, Washington, has an old-fashioned flavor in keeping with the restoration of Seattle's Pioneer Square, but it has all the modern conveniences. (It's about six miles from downtown Seattle.)

Mama Reuben's serves up traditional deli sandwiches, and features two kinds of homemade soups daily. Its bakery produces rye, sourdough, and egg breads, plus four kinds of bagels.

Beer and wine are available, as are take-outs and party trays. It's open from 9 a.m. until 8 p.m. seven days. Closed Thanksgiving, Christmas, and New Year's. 232-4000.

Bluma's B & B Corn Beef House No. 1
103½ Pike
Seattle   624-8173

Humble Herb Mannhalt and his brother Smiley Guen operate Bluma's B
& B Corn Beef House No. 1 at 103½ Pike in downtown Seattle. Bluma
is their mother's name.

Herb says that his place produces a *gemuetlich* atmosphere. It's at the
west side entrance of Seattle's public market, which is being restored.
He also admits to a bit of kibitzing with the customers.

The B & B does a big lunch business, serving home-cooked meat
sandwiches on its home-baked rye bread. Also homemade are soups,
salads, and strudel. And there are six tons of home-processed dills in
storage.

Catering and take-outs, but no beer or wine. The B & B is open from
9 a.m. to 7 p.m. Monday through Saturday. Closed Rosh Hashanah,
Yom Kippur, Memorial Day, and Christmas. 624-8173.

WEST VIRGINIA

Ray's Deli
200 - 35th Street S.E.
Charleston   925-0211

Ray's Deli, 200 - 35th Street S.E., Charleston, West Virginia, is noted
for its homemade carrot cake. More than 23,000 have been sold.

Ray's combines a sit-down and take-out deli and a gourmet food
shop. Choose from standard sandwiches, homemade soups and salads, or
one of the special combo sandwiches. They're tagged with such names as
"Almost Heaven," "Cruel Blue," and "Yachtsman." Beer is served.

Hours are 9 a.m. - 10 p.m. seven days a week, but closed on Rosh
Hashanah and Yom Kippur. 925-0211.

Lanos-Kraus Delicatessen
68 - 12th Street
Wheeling   232-9172

Lanos-Kraus Delicatessen is a take-out establishment in downtown Wheeling, West Virginia at 68 - 12th Street. Lunch business is especially brisk.

Mr. Lanos purveys imported foods, homemade chicken by the pound, sausages, salads, Reuben and other sandwiches, and fish. Imported and domestic beers are available.

Lanos does custom catering, and numbers West Virginia pol Jay Rockefeller among his customers. The place is open from 8 a.m. 'til 9:30 p.m. six days. Closed Sundays and holidays. 232-9172.

WISCONSIN

Benjamin's Restaurant and Delicatessen
4160 Oakland Ave.
Milwaukee   332-7777

Home cooking (with corned beef featured) is the specialty of Benjamin's Restaurant and Delicatessen, 4160 Oakland Ave, Milwaukee.

Benjamin's emphasizes its hot meals, serves beer and wine, and does catering. It's open from 7 - 8 seven days. (Closed holidays.) 332-7777.

International Sandwich Shoppe
739 N. 16th St.
Milwaukee   933-1314

Across the street from the Marquette University dorms at 739 North 16th Street in Milwaukee is a place designed for sandwich-hungry students, faculty, visitors, tourists who crave food after touring the breweries, and even indigenous personnel. It's the International Sandwich Shoppe.

The ISS is almost exclusively take-out, but there are a couple of benches where you can partake if you're really starved. Choose from all kinds of submarines (turkey is the favorite; it comes with lettuce, tomato, mayo and your choice of cheeses).

Another biggie is steak sandwiches, but that's not really a deli item, so maybe you'd rather have the Traveler's. On a scooped-out half loaf of

French bread you get ground beef, onions, mozzarella *et al.* heated and melted together. If meat turns you off, ISS has a Vegetarian — a variety of cheeses melted down with lettuce and tomato and served on a Kaiser roll. Getting back to meat, you can also have standards such as salami, meatball, and bologna subs. Also many bagel combos.

The Shoppe make its own desserts and features baklava. Get healthy again with a fresh mango shake.

The International Sandwich Shoppe is open Monday through Thursday from 11 - 2; 'til 3 on Friday; 4 on Saturday, and it's open from 3 - 2 on Sunday. 933-1314.

Jake's Delicatessen
1634 W. North Ave.
Milwaukee   562-1272

For a trip into the recent past, try Jake's Delicatessen at 1634 West North Avenue in Milwaukee. The fixtures date back to 1946, and the business itself is about 45 years old.

Owner Irv Kassof says that kosher corned beef is his top specialty, and he also recommends his homemade soup and short ribs. Beer and wine are served.

Jake's is open from 9 - 5:30 six days. (Closed Sundays and Jewish holidays.) 562-1272.

WYOMING

Our Kitchen
Box 1412
(one block off the square)
Jackson   733-6446

You can't see the Grand Tetons from Our Kitchen in Jackson. The view is obstructed by a butte. However, Our Kitchen is a beaut of a deli, and you can stoke up there before going out to admire the scenery. Or afterwards, if you prefer. Or both.

Owner Joan Richards describes the decor of her establishment as "Western Bavarian," which befits the mountainous surroundings. During the summer, Our Kitchen is open around-the-clock. Breakfast, featuring sourdough pancakes and omelettes, is served from 11 p.m. 'til 11 a.m.

Year-round lunch features a special sandwich of the day plus classic deli favorites, submarine sandwiches, and homemade soups. During the summer, sandwiches are available at all hours, and dinners are served from 5 p.m. until 10 p.m. A favorite is baked trout. No alcoholic beverages are served, but Wyoming law permits you to bring your own. Occasionally, natural-food specials are offered.

Our Kitchen also incorporates a deli shop that features imported meats and cheeses. It does a brisk box-lunch business in the summer. (Jackson is a gateway to Grand Teton and Yellowstone National Parks.) Winter sports devotees are not neglected. Nearby areas for snowbunnies include Jackson Hole and Snow King Mountain.

As noted, Our Kitchen is open 24 hours daily in the summer. At other times it may be open for lunch only or during daylight hours. Check by calling 733-6446.

Deli on the Tracks
100 Ivinson Avenue
Laramie   742-2238

Git along little dogie and make tracks for the Deli on the Tracks in downtown Laramie at 100 Ivinson Avenue.

Take in the unique intimate atmosphere garnished with plants and listen to the mellow pop and classical background music. Try something special. Although traditional deli sandwiches are available, the Deli on the Tracks is natural-oriented. A couple of its special sandwiches are tomato and avocado, and alfalfa sprouts and cheese.

Home cooking and baking are featured. There's a different soup each day, and desserts include cheesecake and baklava. But no alcoholic beverages are served.

If you're off to round up your herd, you can have a picnic lunch prepared. You don't have to be a cowboy, though. It's a popular place for all kinds of tenderfeet, including students from the nearby University of Wyoming.

The Deli on the Tracks is open from 11 a.m. until 7 p.m. Monday through Saturday. Closed Sundays and major holidays. 742-2238.

6 Deli Food Recipes (Or, Beyond the Corned Beef on Rye)

What is a book on delicatessens without recipes using deli foods? Almost everyone has tasted, at one time or another, a bagel with cream cheese or a ham-and-cheese-on-an-onion-roll with a kosher dill on the side. But for those fans who have never had the pleasure of whipping up a homemade matzo ball or creating the world's *best* sandwich single-handedly, the recipes that follow should open up a whole new world of cuisine.

Selections include tried-and-true traditional deli favorites plus some real innovations using customary deli ingredients. A deli meal doesn't have to be a cold sandwich or a platter of salads and cold cuts. The recipes contained in this chapter attempt to go beyond the corned-beef-on-rye, revealing the secrets of those old favorites and broadening the horizons of the carry-out deli shopper.

Contributions were made by veteran deli proprietors, deli-food manufacturers and some personal friends who (sometimes under duress) parted with old family secrets.

Thanks go to them all for bringing the irresistible aromas and flavors of the corner deli into the American kitchen.

Appetizers

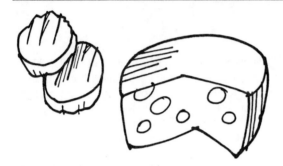

CHEESE BOBS

1 8-oz. package cream cheese
1 tsp. finely chopped onion
1 tsp. Worcestershire sauce
1 4-oz. package corned beef, finely chopped

Combine cheese, onion and Worcestershire sauce. Form into small, bite-sized balls and roll in chopped corned beef.
Makes about 36 cheese balls

CORNUCOPIAS

1 cup cottage cheese, sieved
1 tsp. prepared horseradish or mustard
1 T. salad dressing
2 4-oz. packages corned beef

Combine cottage cheese, horseradish or mustard, and salad dressing. Spread on 3-inch strips of corned beef and roll to resemble horns of plenty. Garnish with parsley sprigs.

LOX ROLLS

Lox
Cream Cheese
Horseradish or chopped cucumber

Slice lox into 1-inch strips. Season cream cheese with horseradish or peeled, chopped cucumber to taste. Spread lox strips with cream cheese mixture, roll up and serve on toothpicks.

PICKLED HERRING APPETIZER

Boston lettuce
Minced onion
Cole slaw
Pickled herring
Sour cream

Arrange lettuce leaves on salad plates. Spoon layer of finely minced onion over lettuce and top with layer of cole slaw. Spoon pickled herring over cole slaw and pour sour cream over all. Serve well chilled.

SALAMI PICKLEWICHES

Dill pickles
Salami
Swiss cheese

Cut large dill pickles in half lengthwise. Cut two pieces salami and one piece Swiss cheese to size and shape of pickle. Place cheese between slices of salami and insert in pickles, sandwich fashion. Chill.

STUFFED CELERY

1/4 tsp. Worcestershire sauce
1/2 cup cottage cheese
1/3 cup chopped sweet gherkins
1/4 tsp. salt
1 T. chopped celery leaves
6 celery stalks, cut in 8-inch pieces

Combine Worcestershire, cottage cheese, gherkins, salt and celery leaves; mix well. Spread cheese mixture on celery stalks.
6 Servings (only about 29 calories each)

Salads

POTATO SALAD WITH PICKLED HERRING

2 cups potatoes cooked, cooled and chopped
1 cup pickled herring, chopped
1 cup chopped celery
2 T. minced parsley and/or chives
1/2 cup sour cream
1½ T. lemon juice
1/2 tsp. cayenne or paprika

Toss all ingredients in salad bowl and chill. Serve on lettuce leaves.
6 Servings

POTATO SALAD ZUM ZUM

8 medium unpared potatoes, washed and halved
2 cans (10½ ounces each) beef consomme
Water
8 slices bacon
2 medium onions, chopped
Salad oil
2/3 cup white vinegar
1 T. Dijon mustard
1 T. sugar
1 T. salt
1/2 tsp. white pepper
1 cup chopped parsley

Place potatoes and consomme in saucepan or Dutch oven; add enough water to cover. Simmer 20 minutes or until fork-tender. Drain; peel and slice potatoes. Saute bacon until crisp; remove and crumble. In bacon drippings, saute onions until crisp-tender. Remove with slotted spoon. Add enough salad oil to bacon drippings to measure 1/3 cup. Combine with vinegar. In same skillet, stir vinegar mixture into mustard, sugar, salt and pepper; blend and heat to boiling. Pour over potatoes, bacon and onion; add 3/4 cup parsley. Toss lightly. Garnish with remaining parsley. Serve warm.
Makes 2 quarts

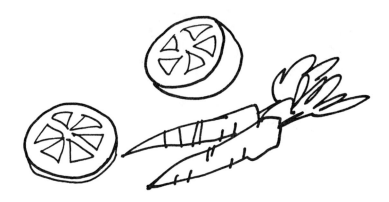

COUNTRY KITCHEN MACARONI SALAD

1 T. salt
3 quarts boiling water
2 cups elbow macaroni (8 ounces)
1/2 cup grated carrot
1/2 cup chopped cucumber
1/2 cup chopped celery
1/4 cup chopped green pepper
1/2 cup mayonnaise
1 T. prepared mustard
1 tsp. salt
1/4 tsp pepper

Add 1 tablespoon salt to rapidly boiling water. Gradually add macaroni so that water continues to boil. Cook uncovered, stirring occasionally, until tender. Drain; rinse with cold water and drain.

Combine macaroni with remaining ingredients. Toss lightly but thoroughly. Chill. Garnish with parsley if desired.
4 to 6 Servings

ITALIAN SALAD

1/2 lb. sliced olive loaf
2 cups shell macaroni, cooked, drained and cooled
1/4 cup chopped celery
1/4 cup green pepper, thinly sliced
1 tomato, cut in 8 wedges
2 T. scallions, finely chopped
1/4 cup Italian salad dressing
1/4 cup mayonnaise

Chop meat coarsely, add remaining ingredients and toss lightly. Serve on lettuce leaves.
6 Servings

BASIC COLE SLAW

6 cups finely shredded cabbage
1 cup shredded carrot
1/3 cup undrained sweet pickle relish
1 T. grated onion
3/4 cup mayonnaise
1/2 tsp. salt
1/4 tsp. celery seed
1/8 tsp. pepper
1/8 tsp. dry mustard

Combine all ingredients; toss lightly. Chill. Garnish with pickle fan, if desired.
6 to 8 Servings (about 5 cups)

Sandwiches

ROUND REUBEN

2 cups drained sauerkraut
1/2 tsp. caraway or dill seed
1/8 tsp. garlic powder
16 slices round bread
1/2 cup Russian dressing
1 lb. thinly sliced corned beef
1 pound natural Swiss cheese in rectangular slices
Melted butter or margarine

Toss kraut with caraway seed and garlic powder; set aside. Spread bread
with dressing. Top 8 bread slices with corned beef, kraut, cheese and
remaining 8 bread slices. Brush melted butter on both sides of sandwiches. Grill in skillet or electric sandwich toaster until cheese is melted.
8 Servings

DILLY CLUB SANDWICHES

1/4 lb. sliced cooked corned beef
12 slices white bread, toasted
1/2 cup sliced dill pickles
2 T. mayonnaise
4 slices cooked turkey
4 slices tomato
Crisp lettuce leaves
Salt and pepper to taste

Arrange corned beef on 4 slices bread. Top with dill pickles and 4 slices bread. Spread bread with mayonnaise. Top with turkey, tomato slices and lettuce. Sprinkle with salt and pepper and top with remaining 4 slices bread. Secure with cocktail picks.
4 Servings

DOUBLE CLUB SANDWICH

24 slices white bread, crusts removed
6 slices American sheese
3/4 cup thinly sliced dill pickles
1 3-ounce package cream cheese, softened
1 T. sweet pickle liquid (drained from sweet mixed pickles)
6 slices cooked chicken or turkey
6 slices cooked ham
1/4 cup mayonnaise
1/4 cup sweet mixed pickles, drained and chopped
Dill pickles, halved lengthwise (optional)

On 6 bread slices, arrange cheese and sliced pickles; top each with another bread slice. Combine cream cheese and sweet pickle liquid and blend until smooth; spread on bread; top with chicken slices. Cover chicken with another bread slice, then ham. Combine mayonnaise and chopped sweet mixed pickles; spread over ham and top with remaining bread. Garnish with additional pickles, if desired.
6 Servings

GOURMET TURKEY SANDWICH

4 slices rye bread
Butter
4 slices Swiss cheese
1 package smoked sliced turkey (about 4 oz.)
4 slices tomato
1 small head lettuce, shredded
Russian or Thousand Island dressing
Stuffed olives (optional)

Spread bread with butter. Place 1 slice on each serving plate. Top with Swiss cheese, turkey and tomato slice. Heap with lettuce and spoon dressing over all. Garnish with olives, if desired.
4 Servings

STACK-THE-DECK SANDWICH

2 cups well-drained sauerkraut (about 16 ounces undrained weight)
3 T. salad oil
1/2 cup shredded carrot
3/4 cup chopped sweet pickle
1 tsp. salt
1/8 tsp. pepper
1 lb. loaf pumpernickel bread, about 8 inches long
3 T. softened butter or margarine
Crisp romaine lettuce leaves
4 large thin tomato slices
1/2 lb. sliced Swiss cheese
1/4 lb. sliced turkey loaf
1/4 lb. sliced corned beef

Several hours before serving, mix kraut, oil, carrot, pickle and seasonings in a bowl; cover and chill.

Trim bottom crust from loaf of bread. Cut bread into 3 horizontal slices; spread cut surfaces lightly with butter. On bottom third of bread, layer half of the romaine, tomato slices, Swiss cheese, turkey loaf, corned beef and kraut mixture. Add second bread slice; layer remaining ingredients on bread. Cover with top of bread. Secure with skewers or large picks.
4 to 6 Servings

SANDWICH-IN-THE-ROUND

1 3-oz. package cream cheese, softened
1/3 cup mayonnaise
2 tsp. prepared mustard
1 12-oz. can luncheon meat, diced
1/4 cup chopped sweet gherkins
1 unsliced round loaf pumpernickel bread
1 large tomato, sliced
4 slices bacon, cooked and crumbled

Blend cheese, mayonnaise and mustard. Add meat and pickles; mix well. Cut bread lengthwise into three layers. Spread half meat mixture on bottom layer of bread. Top with second layer of bread. Spread remaining meat mixture on bread. Top with tomato, bacon and remaining bread layer. Chill. Cut into quarters.
4 Servings

TWIN HIGH BOY KRAUTWICHES

1 5-oz. jar pasteurized process blue cheese spread
1 12-oz. can beer
2 cups well-drained sauerkraut (about 16 ounces)
1/2 cup chopped radishes
3 T. finely chopped parsley
1/4 tsp. seasoned salt
Dash of freshly ground black pepper
1 round loaf pumpernickel bread, about 6 inches in diameter
Lettuce leaves
1/2 lb. sliced cooked ham
1/2 lb. cooked beef salami
Radish roses for garnish
Pickles for garnish

Combine blue cheese spread and 2 tablespoons of the beer; set aside.
Place the remaining beer and sauerkraut in a saucepan and simmer,
uncovered, about 5 minutes; cool completely. Drain thoroughly and add
radishes, parsley, seasoned salt and pepper; toss to blend seasonings.
    Cut bread horizontally into 6 slices. Spread blue cheese mixture on
all cut surfaces. For each krautwich, use 3 slices of bread. Score bottom
and top crusts into quarters for easier cutting. On first slice of bread
place lettuce, quarter of kraut mixture, quarter of the ham slices and
quarter of the salami slices; add second slice of bread and repeat
lettuce, kraut and cold meat layers. Top with third slice of bread.
Repeat, making another krautwich. Wrap and chill krautwiches about 1
hour before serving. Garnish with radish roses and pickles. Cut each
krautwich into quarters for serving.
8 Servings

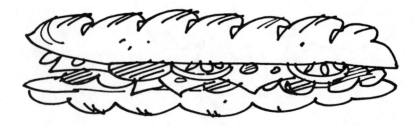

BRATWURST SANDWICH

1 lb. precooked Bratwurst
1 can sauerkraut
Hard rolls
Catsup or chili sauce

Cook bratwurst in pot with sauerkraut until both are heated thoroughly.
Place bratwurst on roll and top with a spoonful or two of sauerkraut.
Top off with catsup or chili sauce.
4 to 6 Servings

BOLOGNA FINGER SANDWICHES

1 lb. sliced bologna
1 lb. sliced process American cheese
8 frankfurter rolls, split and buttered
8 sweet gherkins, sliced lengthwise
1/3 cup chili sauce

Halve slices of bologna and cheese; place 2 half-slices cheese on the roll
halves. Arrange strips of gherkins on cheese; top with bologna. Spread
chili sauce over each sandwich. Broil 3 to 4 inches from source of heat,
until cheese is melted and rolls and bologna are slightly browned.

SUPER SANDWICH

Large loaf Italian bread (about 15 inches long)
1/4 cup prepared mustard
16 slices salami
3 T. well drained, sweet pickle relish
16 slices sweet fresh cucumber pickles
8 slices process American cheese, halved diagonally
Parsley

Cut bread into 8 equal pieces. Slice each piece in half, taking care not
to cut all the way through; spread with mustard. Place 2 salami slices
(folded in half and filled with pickle relish), 2 pickle slices and a cheese
triangle in each piece to form sandwich. Arrange sandwiches to form
loaf. If desired, wrap in aluminum foil; bake in hot (400-degree) oven 10
minutes. Garnish with parsley.
8 Servings

Main Dishes

MINI-MAC

1 loaf Italian bread (15 inches long)
Softened butter or margarine
1/2 cup mayonnaise
1 T. prepared mustard
1/3 cup finely chopped onion
1/2 cup sliced pimiento-stuffed olives
2 cups well-drained sauerkraut (about 16 ounces undrained weight)
Salt and pepper
6 ounces thinly sliced salami
6 ounces imitation chicken loaf
Whole pimiento-stuffed olives, for garnish

Cut the top third off bread; scoop out the soft interior of bottom part.*
Spread interior of top and bottom with butter. Score bread into 4
sections for easier cutting when serving. Blend mayonnaise and mustard
in large bowl; add onion, sliced olives and kraut. Toss mixture until
combined well, then season to taste with salt and pepper.

Line bottom of loaf with two-thirds of salami and chicken loaf slices;
fill with kraut mixture. Top kraut with reamining meat slices. Replace
top of bread and insert skewers in bread for easier slicing. If desired,
garnish skewers with whole olives.
*Use soft center for bread crumbs in stuffing.
4 to 6 Servings

FRANK AND KRAUT CHILI BAKE

1 lb. frankfurters
2 T. salad oil
2 medium onions, thinly sliced
1 T. flour
1/4 cup catsup
2 T. vinegar
1/4 cup firmly packed dark brown sugar
2 tsp. Worcestershire
1/4 tsp chili powder
1¼ tsp. salt
Pepper to taste
2½ cups sauerkraut, undrained

Cut frankfurters diagonally into quarters. Saute in hot oil in large skillet until browned. Remove and set aside. In same skillet, saute onions until tender. Blend in flour. Add remaining ingredients; mix well and stir until mixture comes to a boil. Layer the kraut mixture with the frankfurters in a 2½ quart casserole. Cover casserole and bake in moderate (350-degree) oven 30 minutes.
4 Servings

CORNED BEEF DINNER RING

1 T. prepared mustard
1 cup soft bread crumbs
2 T. chopped onion
2 T. chopped green pepper
2 T. melted butter
1/8 tsp. black pepper
1 4-oz. package corned beef, chopped
3/4 cup evaporated milk
1/4 cup water
2 eggs, slightly beaten

Combine all ingredients and mix thoroughly. Pour into well greased, 1-quart ring mold. Place mold in pan of hot water and bake in moderate oven (350 degrees F.) about 30 minutes, or until knife inserted in center comes out clean. Fill center of mold with vegetables or salad greens. Delicious hot or cold.
4 to 6 Servings

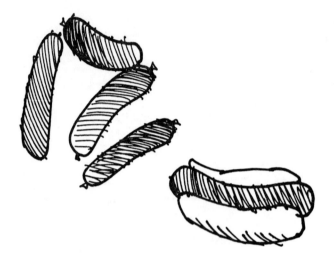

THE ABE GOLD HOT DOG CASSEROLE

6 pure-beef hot dogs
2 cups Creamettes
1 can peas
1 can cream of mushroom soup
4 slices American cheese

Boil 2 cups of Creamettes in water until they are soft. Put Creamettes in lightly greased casserole. Add peas. Cut up hot dogs in bite-sized pieces and put in casserole, mixing them with peas and Creamettes so they will not be in one spot. Add cream of mushroom soup. Put about 4 slices of American cheese on top and bake in 350 degree oven for half and hour. Serve with French bread and salad.
4 to 6 Servings

APPLE SAUERKRAUT WITH POTATO PANCAKES

1 lb. frankfurters, cut in quarters crosswise
1/4 cup butter or margarine
1/2 cup chopped onion
2 cups chopped, cored (unpeeled) red apple
2 T. dark brown sugar
1 tsp. salt
1/8 tsp. pepper
1 tsp. caraway seed
3¼ cups drained sauerkraut
Potato Pancakes*

Fry frankfurters in butter until browned on all sides. Remove and set aside. Add onion and saute until golden; add franks and all remaining ingredients except pancakes. Cook about 5 minutes or until kraut mixture is hot throughout. Heap in warm serving dish. Serve with Potato Pancakes.
6 Servings

*Potato Pancakes:
Beat 3 eggs, 1½ teaspoons salt and 1/8 teaspoon pepper in large bowl. Add 1/4 cup chopped onion, 2 tablespoons chopped parsley, 1/3 cup unsifted flour, 1/4 teaspoon baking powder and 5 medium potatoes (about 1¾ pounds) that have been pared and shredded; stir just until ingredients are mixed. Melt about 2 tablespoons butter in large skillet; pour about 3 tablespoons batter into skillet for each pancake. Immediately flatten mound of batter with tines of fork. Fry pancakes on each side until golden brown; drain on paper towels. Keep warm. Add more butter to skillet as needed.
Makes 18 four-inch pancakes

SMOPOPANS

5 medium potatoes, pared
2 eggs, well beaten
1 package smoked sliced beef, cut up (about 4 oz.)
1/2 cup flour
1 tsp. baking powder
Butter or bacon drippings
Applesauce

Grate raw potatoes and squeeze dry; stir into eggs. Add beef. Sift together flour and baking powder; stir into potato mixture. Lightly grease griddle or frying pan with butter or bacon drippings. Drop batter by spoonfuls onto hot griddle; brown on both sides. Serve hot with chilled applesauce.
5 to 6 Servings

CORNED BEEF BLINTZES

1 egg
1/2 tsp. salt
1 cup water
1 cup flour
1 cup cottage cheese
1 4-oz. package corned beef, chopped
1/2 cup sour cream

Beat egg with fork to blend well. Add salt and water. Sift flour and stir into batter, mixing until smooth. Grease a frying pan about 6 inches in diameter, heat it well and pour in 2 T. of the batter, tilting the pan to allow batter to run over the bottom. Cook over low heat on one side only, until pancake holds its shape. Turn out on a clean cloth and repeat with remaining batter. Combine cottage cheese and corned beef. Spread about 1/4 cup on each pancake and fold. Cook in butter or margarine until heated through. Serve with a garnish of sour cream and a little chopped corned beef.
Makes 8 blintzes

PARK AVENUE CABBAGE

3 T. butter
3 T. flour
1/2 tsp. salt
1-1/3 cups milk
1 package smoked sliced beef, cut up (about 4 oz.)
3 cups cooked chopped cabbage
1 cup soft bread crumbs
Butter or margarine

Melt 3 tablespoons butter; blend in flour and salt. Add milk and cook, stirring constantly, until thickened. Add beef and cabbage; pour into greased, 1½ quart casserole. Top with crumbs and dot with butter. Bake in 350 degree oven for 25 minutes.
4 Servings

STUFFED FRANKWURST

4 giant-sized frankwurst
2 cups dry packaged stuffing mix
2/3 cup water
1 egg
6 T. butter or margarine
Finely chopped celery and onion (optional)
American cheese and bacon (optional)

Slice frankwurst in half lengthwise. Melt butter or margarine in sauce pan. Saute onions and celery and add moistened stuffing mix. Place stuffing on one half of each frankwurst. Replace top half of frankwurst and secure with toothpicks. Wrap in aluminum foil, allowing toothpicks to push through foil. For change of taste, use strips of bacon or, for variety, use slices of American cheese cut lengthwise and wrap around frankwurst, securing with toothpicks. Place in shallow baking pan. Bake for 25-30 minutes at 350 degrees F.
4 Servings

COLD CUT OMELET

1/4 lb. sliced cold cuts, such as ham, old-fashioned loaf, or ham and cheese loaf
1/4 cup butter
8 eggs, beaten
1/4 cup milk
1/2 tsp. salt
Pepper to taste

Dice cold cuts. Saute over low heat in omelet pan (9 inches) for 2 to 3 minutes. Remove and set aside meat. Blend eggs, milk and seasonings and pour into pan. Cook over low heat, and as eggs set, lift with spatula and allow uncooked portion to flow under them. Spoon meat into center of eggs. When eggs are completely set, fold omelet sides into center.
4 Servings

CORNED BEEF EN CASSEROLE WITH POTATO CRUST

3 T. butter or margarine
3 T. flour
1 tsp. salt
1/4 tsp. pepper
1/4 tsp. chopped parsley
1 tsp. chopped onion
1½ cups meat stock, heated
2 4-oz. packages corned beef, chopped
1½ cups diced assorted cooked vegetables
Potato crust

Melt butter, add flour, seasonings and 1/3 cup hot meat stock. Blend well. Add remaining stock gradually and cook until thickened. Mix all ingredients and put in lightly greased casserole. Top with potato crust.

POTATO CRUST

2 cups sifted, all-purpose flour
1/2 tsp. salt
2 tsp. baking powder
1/2 cup shortening
1 cup cold mashed potatoes
Milk or water

Sift together flour, salt and baking powder. Cut in shortening. Add mashed potatoes and enough milk or water to hold together like pie crust. Place on top of corned beef mixture and slash top in several places. Bake in a hot oven (375-degrees F.) about 20 minutes, or until browned on top.
4 to 6 Servings

Old Favorites

Abe Lebewohl, proprietor of the 2nd Avenue Delicatessen—Restaurant in New York, has written his own cookbook, which at this writing is due to be published. Here is his "Essen Lesson" for matzo balls:

ABE LEBEWOHL'S MATZO BALLS

5 eggs
3/4 tsp. baking powder
1/2 cup onion-flavored oil
Salt and pepper
2 cups Matzo meal

For 12 matzo balls, beat 5 eggs, by mixer or by hand, but mix well. Add 3/4 teaspoonful of baking powder and a half cup onion-flavored oil.* Add salt and pepper. Combine all ingredients and beat well. Take 2 cups of Matzo meal, pour little by little into the egg mixture and continue until all is used and the mix is of a thick consistency. Boil a pot of water which holds a pinch of salt. Take a soup spoon, wet your hands and put a scoop of the dough into your palms. Roll it, one hand almost against the other. (If you use an ice cream scoop, you won't need this last tactic because you will form perfect matzo balls without it.)
    Gently submerge each ball into the boiling water and boil for 20 to 30 minutes (over-boiling will not hurt).
Good Luck.
*Oil (preferably soybean) fried in onions and strained. (Do not add water.)
Makes 12 matzo balls

Some of his friends say that Bob Protzel (humor writer and proprietor of Protzel's Delicatessen in Clayton, Missouri) has a lot of schmaltz. He has kindly consented to share his recipe for same, along with a couple of other classics that follow:

SCHMALTZ (RENDERED CHICKEN FAT)

5 lbs. raw chicken fat
2 small onions, peeled and sliced

Boil together fat and onions until fat is liquefied and onions are quite brown. Strain to remove onion bits and solid pieces of unrendered fat. Pour strained fat into jars and refrigerate until needed. Will solidify under refrigeration and remain fresh indefinitely. Schmaltz makes a delicious seasoning for fresh cooked or canned vegetables, and savory shortening for frying. Remaining onion bits and crisped bits of fat, when well drained, are delicious but rather indigestible snacks, and also can be used as seasonings in all types of dishes. The crisped bits of fat are known as "gribbenehs."

MY YIDDISHE MAMA'S AROMATIC, SAVORY, DELUXE BREAKFAST TOAST

1- to 4-day old, sliced Jewish rye bread
Schmaltz
Fresh garlic clove
Bermuda onions or black radishes
Salt

Toast rye bread slices. When toasted, rub crust with peeled garlic clove. Spread liberally with schmaltz. Cover with either peeled onion slices or peeled black radish slices. Serve with hot tea or coffee. Absolutely delicious. May be followed immediately by spasmodic burping period. To avoid, take either several glasses "grepz water" (seltzer), antacid, or coat stomach lining with one of those stomach-lining products advertised on television. Prayer may not help, but it certainly won't hurt.
CAUTION: Avoid breathing in the direction of anyone whose friendship you would like to retain.

The following old family recipe was donated by Honest Lawyer Herb Lowinger, a dedicated chopped liver maven. According to Herb, the directions must be followed *explicitly* to come up with the genuine item. Please don't add mayonnaise.

CHOPPED CHICKEN LIVER

Butter
1 lb. chicken livers
1 tsp. salt
1/2 tsp. onion or garlic salt
3 heaping T. schmaltz (chicken fat)
2 hard-cooked eggs

Saute chicken livers in butter just until cooked through. Put through a meat grinder (coarse setting) and then chop again by hand ("No blender! We do *not* want a pate!"). Add seasonings, then schmaltz and chopped eggs.

KASHA KNISHES

5 T. butter
1½-2 chopped onions
1/2 lb. fresh mushrooms
1/4 tsp. dried thyme
1/4 tsp. dillweed
Salt and pepper
2 cups cooked kasha

2½ cups flour
1 tsp. double-acting baking powder
1/2 tsp. salt
2 eggs
1/2 cup vegetable oil
2-3 T. water

For the kasha filling, saute onion in melted butter. Clean mushrooms and chop coarsely. Stir onions and seasonings into pan with onions, adding salt and pepper to taste. Saute mixture 5 to 10 minutes. Add kasha to pan and stir; cook over medium heat until mixture is heated well.

For the dough, sift together flour, baking powder and salt. Put in large bowl and add eggs, oil and water. Mix and knead dough with your hands until the dough is smooth.

Roll dough out as thinly as possible and cut out 3-inch circles. Place a large spoonful of filling on each circle and pull dough edges over filling; seal well. Arrange knishes on greased baking sheet with the sealed sides up and bake in 375 degree oven about 1/2 hour, or until light brown.

Makes 18 knishes

POTATO PANCAKES

2 cups potatoes, grated
3 eggs, beaten well
4 tsp. flour
1 tsp. salt
1 tsp. to 1 T. grated onion (optional)
4 T. or more shortening or oil
Applesauce

Peel and grate potatoes and wring out moisture in a towel or cloth. Put potatoes in bowl with eggs, and stir. Sift together flour and salt and add to bowl. Add grated onion, if desired. Shape potato mixture into patties about 1/4-inch thick, heat oil in skillet and cook patties until brown and crisp on both sides. Serve immediately with applesauce.
Makes 12 pancakes

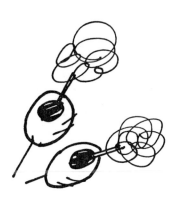

GEFILTE FISH

3 lbs. skinned and boned fish
4 large onions
1 egg, beaten well
1/4 cup matzo meal
3/4 cup cold water
1 tsp. salt
1/2 tsp. pepper
2 carrots
Salt and pepper

For the fish, use whatever kind your grandmother used — maybe buffalo, pike or carp. Especially carp. Gefilte fish authorities say that you have to use at least a little bit of carp to give it the right taste. Put fish and 3 onions through fine blade of food grinder or in blender. Place in bowl with egg, matzo meal, cold water, salt and pepper. Mix until light and fluffy.

Make fish stock with heads, bones and skins of fish. Place in large kettle and cover with water. Add remaining onion, sliced; carrots, sliced thinly, and salt and pepper to taste. Bring stock to a boil. Form fish mixture into balls, wetting hands if necessary. Drop balls into boiling fish stock and simmer, covered, for about 2 hours. Remove the fish balls and serve with a sauce made from strained stock thickened with egg yolks.

CHALE

1 package dry yeast
1 T. sugar
1¼ cups lukewarm water
5 cups (approx.) white flour
2 tsp. salt
2 eggs
2 T. melted shortening
1 egg yolk
Poppy seeds

Dissolve yeast in 1/4 cup of the lukewarm water (water should be around 80 degrees F; if it is too cool, it will not activate yeast; if too hot, the yeast will die). Add the sugar. Sift into bowl 4 to 4½ cups of the flour and the salt. Add eggs, shortening, 1 cup lukewarm water and yeast. Stir until the dough is mixed well. Turn dough out onto floured board and knead, adding enough of the remaining flour to make an elastic, smooth dough. Put dough into a large greased bowl, cover it with a clean towel or cloth and let it rise for 1 to 1½ hours, until double in bulk. Punch down and let rise again until dough is double in bulk.

Flour board again and divide dough into two pieces, one a little smaller than the other. Pull larger part into 3 equal chunks and roll them into strips. Weave a thick braid with the dough and place on greased baking sheet. Make a smaller braid with the remaining dough and center it on top of the first braid.

Cover the chale dough with a light cloth and let it rise about 30 minutes. Brush the bread with all the yolk and sprinkle poppy seeds over surface. Bake at 375 degrees for 50 minutes, until chale is brown.

VARNISHKES (KASHA AND SHELLS)

8 oz. Shellroni (or macaroni bow ties, pasta squares, etc.)
1 cup kasha (buckwheat groats, either fine, medium or coarse ground)
1/2 tsp. salt
1/2 tsp. pepper
1 T. schmaltz (rendered chicken fat)
1 egg
1 medium onion, peeled and chopped
3 cups water

Cook and drain shells according to directions on box. Mix together
kasha, salt, pepper and raw egg. Spread mixture evenly in pan and place
over low heat until dry (mix occasionally). Brown chopped onion in
schmaltz. Bring water to active boil in separate pot and add kasha
mixture. Cover pot and cook over low heat for approximately 10
minutes, or until water is absorbed (stirring occasionally). Add schmaltz
and onions and cook additional 10 minutes in covered pot over low
heat. Add cooked shells and serve hot as side dish as is, or with beef or
chicken gravy.
Serves 6 to 8 average people or one college-aged son and friend

The following recipe was donated by Max Shapiro of Shapiro's Delicatessen-Cafeteria, Indianapolis, Indiana.

SHAPIRO'S PUMPKIN CAKE

1 18½-oz. package yellow cake mix
1 tsp. cinnamon
1/2 tsp. ground ginger
1/4 tsp. ground nutmeg
2 eggs
1 cup cold water
1½ cups canned pumpkin
1 cup chopped walnuts or pecans
1/4 cup whole white raisins
1/8 cup whole dark raisins
Lemon glaze

Mix. together cake mix, cinnamon, ginger and nutmeg in a large mixing bowl. Blend in eggs and water and beat on medium speed of electric mixer 3 minutes. Beat in pumpkin. Pour into a well greased 9- or 10-inch tube pan. Sprinkle nuts and raisins over batter. With a spoon, gently mix nuts and raisins into batter, being sure none is left on top to burn. "This keeps them suspended," says Shapiro. Bake in a preheated 350-degree oven for 45 minutes. Cool in upright pan 15 minutes. Remove from pan, turn right-side up and continue cooling on wire rack 15 to 20 minutes. Glaze with lemon glaze.

LEMON GLAZE

Grated rind of 1 lemon
Juice of 1 to 1½ lemons
1/2 lb. (approx.) confectioners sugar
1 T. white corn syrup
Chopped walnuts or pecans

Stir together lemon rind, juice and 1 cup confectioners sugar. Stir in corn syrup. Stir in enough additional confectioners sugar to make a glaze consistency. Spread thickly on top of cooled cake, letting glaze drizzle down sides. Sprinkle with chopped nuts. Cool completely and serve.
8 Servings

7 Deli Dictionary Glossary

ENJOY!

A glossary of food terms and other things you may hear or see in a delicatessen. This section alone is worth the price of the book because it can make you a maven.

A

Anchovy — a small fish from which paste is made. Not to be confused with Elmer's Glue.

B

Bagel — not a doughnut with hardening of the arteries. See bagel chapter.

Beblach — beans.

Beef Flanken — short ribs in cabbage soup or boiled with horseradish.

Beef in the Pot — boiled beef with beblach and/or other vegetables.

Bialy, Bialystoker — a flavored muffin that originated in the town of Bialystok, which is near Anatevka.

Blintz — Jewish crepe, usually enfolding cheese or meat, but can be wrapped around fruits or whatever else turns you on. Sour cream is essential with cheese blintzes; jam is optional.

Borscht — an entertainment circuit in the Catskill Mountains. Also a soup — hot or cold; varieties include beet, cabbage (sweet or sour), and beef. Sour cream mandatory with cold beet borscht.

Brisket — a cut of beef that can be served baked or boiled. (Pickled brisket is used for corned beef.)

Bubich, Bubeh (non-diminutive) — literally, a small jewel. Anybody you don't dislike: "Bubileh, have a Cel-Ray on me!"

Bubkis — nothing. As, "This borscht tastes like bubkis."

Bummer — a nogudnik. As Ailene McMahon told the young Eddie Cantor in one of Hollywood's most memorable scenes, "Don't be a bummer."

Challe — egg twist bread. Makes excellent French toast.

Chazer — a pig, a greedy person.

Chazerai — unclean things related to pigs. As in "Don't step in the chazerai, Mr. President." More specifically, junk food.

Cheese — goes between rye bread and corned beef or is wrapped in a blintz.

Chicken in the Pot — see Beef in the Pot and substitute chicken.

Chicken Kiev — not ordinarily found in delis because Kiev is a long way from Anatevka.

Chrayne — horseradish.

Chutzpah — excessive gall, nerve, arrogance. You have chutzpah if you're messing around with your dentist's wife and you let him give you a general anesthetic before an extraction.

Corned Beef — backbone of the delicatessen industry.

Delicatessen — where you go for eppis essen.

Dill — a weed; also a pickle. See pickle chapter.

Dr. Brown's Cel-Ray Tonic — since 1869 a classic celery-flavored beverage accompaniment to deli meats. Manufactured by American Beverage Corp. of College Point, New York, and available in most U.S. metropolitan areas. There is also a franchise bottler in Los Angeles.

Egg Cream — a beverage delicacy seemingly confined to New York. Contains neither egg nor cream. It's a dash chocolate syrup, a dash milk, and a big spritz grepswasser.

Eggs — see Tongue. Also often served in omelette form, as with lox. (See fish chapter.)

Eppis Essen — something to eat in a delicatessen; more than a nosh.

Essen — eating. See fressen.

Fish — see fish chapter.

Frankfurter — also hot dog, wiener, "specials" when they are big (often served with beans). An American sausage with various Austrian and German names. Why people go to ball games besides beer. When served on a roll, sauerkraut and mustard *must* be added.

Fressen — overeating.

Fresser — one who overeats.

Glatt Kosher — food prepared under very strict rabbinical supervision.

Goy — a Gentile. Plural is goyim.

Greps — a burp, belch.

Grepswasser — a carbonated beverage that reduces or produces greps, depending on whether or not you've just eaten, and what you've eaten. See seltzer and two cents plain.

Gribbenehs — crisped bits of fat that remain after schmaltz is rendered. (See recipe.) A nice nosh.

Grits — ground hominy, served only in the South. For one deli that does it, see Atlanta.

Halvah — Turkish-type deli dessert made from sesame. If it's in block form, don't ask what kind of cheese it is or they'll think you're a klutz.

Hamantashen — triangular sweet roll served at Purim, the Feast of Lots.

Hamische — homelike, folksy. "This is a hamische deli." "Yeah, so's the owner's wife."

Heartburn — a common disease contracted in delicatessens. Antidotes and cures include grepswasser.

Helzel — stuffed chicken-neck skin. See kishka.

Horseradish — miracle drug used in treatment of sinusitis.

Ice — what you put in warm Cel-Ray Tonic. (So to make it from **A** to **Z**, we needed an **I**. See also Q, R, U, V and X.)

Jewish K Rations — kasha, kishka, knish, kreplach, kugel.

Kasha — buckwheat groats.

Kasha Varnishkes — kasha with pasta (see recipe.)

Kibby — backbone of the Lebanese delicatessen industry. (See Minneapolis.)

Kibitz — to butt in with gratuitous advice. A kibitzer is the guy at the next table who says, "You should have had the corned beef on white with mayo."

Kishka — a flour base with seasonings and schmaltz stuffed into a piece intestine and served with brown gravy. There's a potato variety, too. Same as stuffed derma.

Klutz — a clod, a bumbler. A guy who falls off the step when leaving the counter at David's, even though the menu says, "Watch your step when leaving counter," and the waitress has already warned him.

Knish — a crusty turnover encasing meat or potato or kasha. Also slang for a pretty girl: "Such a knish!"

Kosher — "clean" or "fit."

Kreplach — Jewish ravioli. Won Ton is Chinese kreplach.

Kugel — it could be noodle or potato, but, "We don't call it 'poojing' anymore." It's a side dish with a meat meal, contains cottage cheese, schmaltz or oil as a binder, sometimes raisins with the noodle version.

Kvell — to glow with pride. "You think your mother's soup is good? Taste *this.*"

Kvetch — to complain, as a verb, or the complainer as a noun. "Don't kvetch about the food; your brother-in-law picked up the check."

Latkes, potato — similar to pancakes, potato.

L'Chaim — a toast "To Life." Cf. "Fiddler on the Roof."

Leching — licking, one of the things not to do in the kitchen. See also fressen and schmeching.

Liver, chicken, chopped — don't make a megillah. See Uncle Herb's recipe. (You want to get fancy, you could call it a pate, but that would cost $1 a pound more, and we don't want that kind of a schmier anyway.)

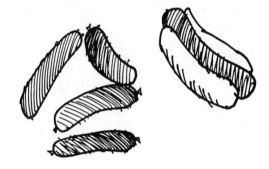

Macher — the boss, an entrepeneur. If you own one delicatessen, you might be considered a maven, but your brother-in-law who owns two is a Deli Macher.

Matzo — unleavened bread used especially during Passover. Unwittingly becomes a binding agent, which is why delis sell so many prunes during Passover.

Matzo Balls — no good for golf, but delicious in chicken soup. See recipe.

Matzo Brei — fried matzo with eggs — a special Passover dish and year-'round breakfast delicacy.

Maven, Mavin, Mayvin — any way you spell it, it means an expert or authority. As in "The Deli Maven is kvetching about the latkes again."

Mazel Tov — "Good Luck." Often used on formal occasions as when you give the Bar Mitzvah his fountain pen.

Megillah — literally, the scroll containing Jewish law. Conversationally akin to "making a mountain out of a molehill." As, "Don't make a megillah because my brother and his family are coming. Send out for some delicatessen."

Mensch — literally "a man," but most often used in the sense of "a nice guy." As in "Would you believe the mensch didn't charge me anything for the lox wings?"

Mishmash — a mixture, mess, jumble. If you put mayonnaise in chopped liver you have a mishmash.

Mishuganer — adj., crazy; n., a crazy. Sometimes followed by "in the kopf."

Mohel — has nothing to do with hand-slicing lox.

Muffuletta — New Orleans' answer to corned beef on rye. See Southern Odyssey chapter.

Mustard — come on, you know.

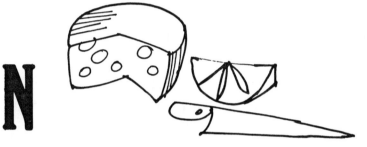

Nebish — a "Poor Soul." An empty cab drives up and a nebish gets out.

Nosh — n., a snack; v., to snack. After a particularly heavy meal, a typical deli owner might tell you it's time to nosh.

Nosherai — a place where you nosh. Or that which you nosh upon.

Oy vayz mir — what you say when you're hungry and the deli is closed.

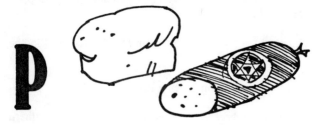

Pareve — food containing neither meat nor milk products, such as gefilte fish.

Pastrami — deckle of brisket cured and seasoned as corned beef, smoked and schmiered with more spices. Originally Romanian, Count Dracula loved it before his tastes changed.

Pepper or peppered beef, meat — shoulder of beef, sometimes in a loaf, spiced like pastrami but leaner.

Phosphate — grepswasser with chocolate, vanilla or fruit flavoring.

Pickle — essential accompaniment (as is mustard) to corned beef or pastrami sandwiches. See pickle chapter.

Pirogen — similar to knishes.

Pucha, also Ptcha — jellied or frozen calves' or cows' feet seasoned. Originated as the most inexpensive meat available to early immigrants. Also known as Instant Garlic.

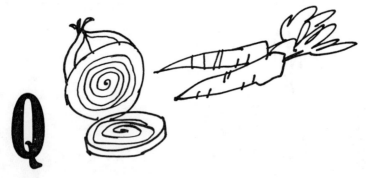

Quince — a fruit you could put in a blintz. Also a borough in New York. See "I."

Radish — second half of "horse." See "I" again.

Salami — uncooked sausage; may be smoked or air-dried.

Sandwich — very large in delis now, but goes way back to John Montagu, the fourth Earl of Sandwich (an English goy, 1718-1792). Legendarily, John had a gambling problem. He would not give up his cards or dice to sit down and drink his chicken soup like his mother wanted him to. Instead, one night when he was working on his 17th pass, he said, "Herbie, just put a piece pastrami between a couple hunks rye bread." That's how *that* all started. Later in America, gamblers and non-gamblers alike developed variations on the Earl's schtick. Today we have not only pastrami and corned beef on rye; we have muffulettas, Po' Boys, grinders, submarines, heroes, even grilled cheese and other mishmashes.

Sauerkraut — shredded cabbage fermented in brine with salt. (In a crock.) Would you have a hot dog without it? See also Zohereh Kraut.

Sausage — smoked and seasoned meat encased in an intestine (but now often plastic-wrapped).

Schadchan — a marriage broker; matchmaker. Sometimes they hang around delicatessens looking for prospects. You maybe have a hamische daughter?

Schlamiel — a waiter who pours soup on a customer.

Schlamazel — the customer on whom the soup is poured.

Schlep — to carry, walk, drag, push, pull.

Schmaltz — rendered chicken fat. See recipe.

Schmeching — smelling: something else you shouldn't do in the kitchen. See fressen and leching.

Schmier — literally "spread," but more likely to be used in expressions such as "He ate the whole schmier."

Schnorer — a beggar, a sponger. They'll call you that if you taste a lot of samples in the deli but don't buy anything.

Schreier — a deli man who screams at customers.

Schtick — something you do well. "What's David's schtick?" "He runs a deli." Henry the Eighth had a couple of schticks — eating and marrying. He didn't need a schadchan.

Seltzer — see grepswasser, two cents plain.

Shav — a drink, usually cold, made from spinach or sour leaves. Sour cream is added.

Sour cream — what you put on blintzes and in shav or borscht.

Stuffed Derma — see kishka.

Tea — a beverage served in a glass.

Tongue — you wouldn't eat what comes out of an animal's mouth? Do you eat eggs?

Traife — unclean, non-kosher food.

Tsorris — troubles, sorrow. "The bagels are stale."

Tuches — what you sit on in a deli or anywhere else.

Two Cents Plain — a small glass grepswasser. Now costs at least five cents.

Ulcer — it shouldn't happen from a decent deli. So see "I" again.

Varnishkes — see kasha, "I" and recipe.

Wurst — German for sausage; also a Jewish word for salami.

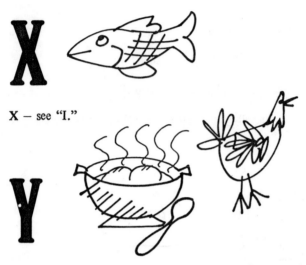

X — see "I."

Yenta — a gossip. They have been known to frequent delis.

Zei Gezuhndt — "Be well"; what you say after a sneeze or greps.

Zoftig — would you believe Shelley Winters?

Zohereh Kraut — sauerkraut, of course.

(Special thanks to gastronomic and linguistic mavens Al Laks, Wally Ginsberg and Simon Wasser, all of Al's Deli in Homewood, Illinois, for their assistance in compiling parts of this section.)

Index to Delis

Deli Notes

Deli Notes

Deli Notes

Deli Notes